Our Favorite Napa Stories

From Wine Country in Shorts

Ralph & Lahni De Amicis

Cuore Libre Publishing
Napa California

Our Favorite Napa Stories
From Wine Country in Shorts
By Ralph & Lahni De Amicis

Published by Cuore Libre Publishing
Napa, California
www.WineCountryInShortscom

Copyright 2025 Ralph & Lahni De Amicis
ISBN 979-8-3485-9905-8
No part of this book may be reproduced in any form without permission from the publisher.

Maps: Ralph De Amicis
Photos Lahni DeAmicis & Ralph DeAmicis

Stage Coach GG Joh Y. Nelson - Public Domain

Contents

Introduction: A Land of Stories 5

Chapter 2: The Power of River Towns 11

Chapter 3: The Romance of the Silverado Trail 19

Chapter 4: Who Named Mount Saint Helena? 27

Chapter 5: Napa's Great Buildings 41

Chapter 6: The Prussians & Italians 55

Chapter 7: Prohibition Changes the Game 81

Chapter 8: Judging California in Far Off Paris 97

Chapter 9: The Mexican Heritage 117

Afterthought: The Fans 127

About the Authors   131

Other Books by the Authors 132

4 Our Favorite Napa Stories

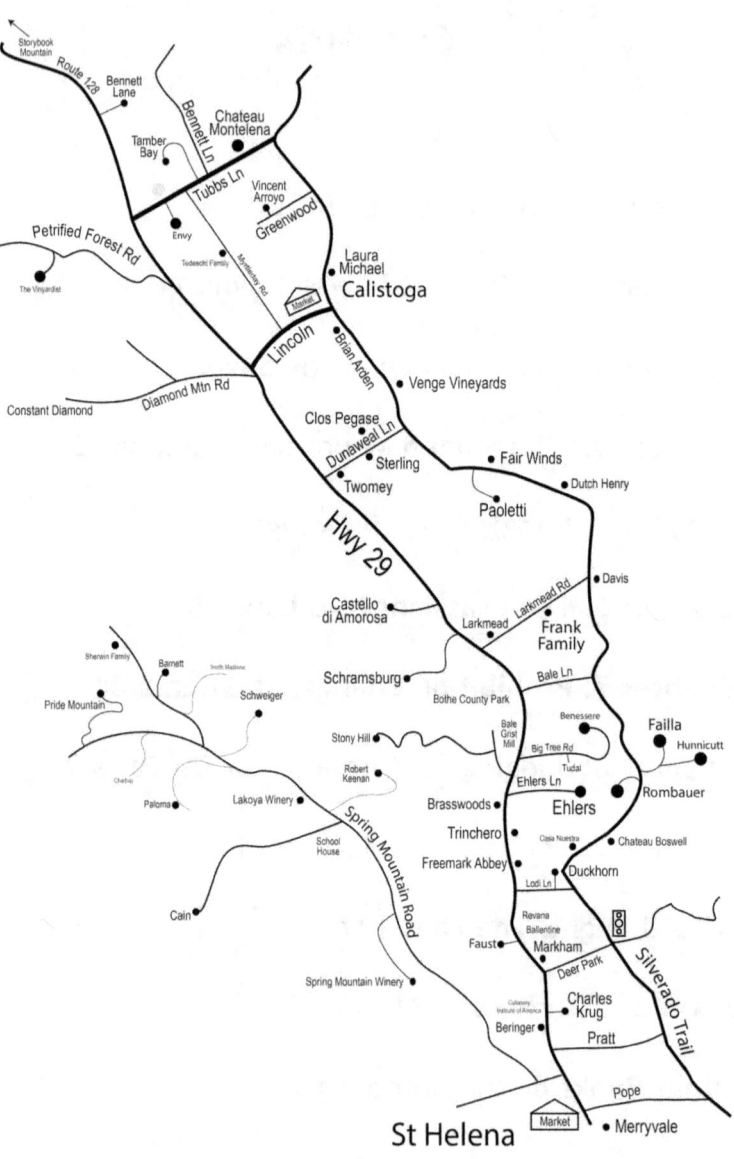

Chapter One
A Land of Stories

This book celebrates the unique storytelling style that goes well with wine: colorful, relaxed, thoughtful, a little rambling and segmented. That's because the pace of the story allows time for the listeners to taste the wines and enjoy the illumination it bestows. That's how the ancients described the experience of drinking alcohol, being illuminated by the wine.' We hope that you enjoy these stories that are only as remarkable as the wonderful places and people they describe, and that are treasured by so many.

A wine region's personality is not just about the topography and climate, but also about how the people living there adapted to its unique qualities. Those experiences are shared in stories. Where did we get these stories? We heard them while standing at the back of countless tasting rooms. For many years there were a couple of hundred wineries where customers could just walk in, stand at the bar and taste the wines. At other wineries the tastings happened sitting down, and of course there are cave and vineyard tours. In these tasting experiences, the hosts shared information about the wines, and many shared stories.

In any given year we visited over three hundred tasting rooms, and we heard so many stories, and multiple versions of those stories! The overall feeling was very casual, relaxed and friendly.

We retold these stories countless times to groups and wine tour clients while driving around the North Bay Wine Country. It was easy to recall those tales when we visited those places where the events occurred. So, to pull together the stories for this book, Ralph started dictating the, into his phone while our clients were tasting at the wineries.

We wanted to write down these stories for a while, but it was hard to find the time. And then a fortuitous thing happened. The local wine tasting fees escalated, and the wineries recognized that if they abandoned their quick tasting bars, in favor of longer seated experiences, their sales would improve.

Honestly, any tour guide could have told them that! The big wines grown in the Napa vineyards taste better when you give them time to open up in the glass. However, as the tastings became more formal, exclusive and expensive, it was a rare time when we stayed with our clients during the sessions.

That scheduling change suddenly gave Ralph a predictable amount of precious, uninterrupted time to dictate the stories, and then later improve the drafts. Choosing the stories was hard becuase an amazing number pop out of his mouth as he drives around with clients. Sometimes he remembers a story because they are passing the winery where a friend first shared it with him.

Many stories have been around so long that there are multiple published versions. For instance, four different people from three groups are credited with naming Mount Saint Helena, the beautiful volcanic cone that towers over Napa Valley.

But, if you keep an open mind, dig deep enough into the research, and account for human nature, you can weave the various versions together into an enjoyable, credible narrative that's pretty close to the truth.

For us, this reweaving happened spontaneously through telling the stories numerous times while noticing both our listeners responses, and whether or not it 'felt' true as we spoke the words. That is a concept from the healing arts, because hearing lies makes us weaker, while hearing the truth makes us stronger!

On the road we've shared these tales with clients in 15 to 20-minute snippets, which is the ideal driving time between wineries, because it allows enough time to metabolize some of the alcohol in preparation for another tasting. But here we've combined those pieces into complete stories, and many turned out to be much longer than we expected.

Even though the stories give us the narrative, in the full version of Wine Country in Shorts, and in our book, A Tour Guide's Napa Valley, we describe the traditions and practices in the winemaking world. These seem to be endlessly interesting to our clients, but that's not surprising.

Two hundred years ago most people worked on the land. Today a tiny fraction of Americans grows everyone else's food and wine, so for most people, this life on the land is far removed from their personal universe. But there must be some deep region within us that still yearns for that ancestral connection to nature.

Is it due to our ancestry, our genetics, or simply our sensual enjoyment of wine, that so many people are drawn to visit the places where it's made? We think the answer to that is 'Yes,' to all of the above! Winemaking is a very elegant type of agriculture that has delightful results.

Visiting Napa is an adventure, although not as risky as it was in the early 1800's when visitors had to contend with the numerous California grizzly bears that lived here. There were so many that outside the region the word Napa meant Bear. We think that's why bravery and audacity are so prized locally, and why Napa attracts so many of the big personalities who show up in these stories from the past and present.

We're sure a scientific study would show that wine tastes better when accompanied by a story, and any story becomes more enjoyable when the wine is good.

Any experienced winery host knows that's true, which is why, as they fill the glasses, the best share stories about the winery's history and location. There's only so much you can say about what's in the glass, because to our bodies, flavor is a language, and great wines have no problem speaking for themselves.

When they tell the story of the struggles involved in clearing the land, planting the vines, building the winery and making a good wine, that connects the guest to that bottle in an emotionally memorable way. Later, when the guest opens the bottle at home, that memory makes the wine taste 'better,' and they have the added pleasure of telling that story to their friends and family.

So, we feel that the best way to enjoy these stories is with a glass of wine in your hand. If you are listening to this as an audio book while driving in a car, we'll give you a pass on that.

Lahni's Editor Note: The Northern California Wine Country is peppered with similar and overlapping stories, many from slightly different perspectives, so you will find that some of the details are repeated, often with a twist that reveals a bit more about the bigger story. So, feel free to dip into the book at any chapter and know that the repetition is intentional, and you will also be better prepared for the Quiz at the end of the book. **(Just kidding, or are we?)**

Chapter One
The Power of River Towns

The first thing you need to understand about Napa is that it's a River Town, because everything starts there. In our modern world when we travel by car, train and plane, much faster than any ship, it's easy to forget how important rivers and waterways have been in the development of societies, cultures and markets. Even today, transporting goods by ship is dramatically more efficient compared to every other method. Americans think of our country as special and, in many ways, it is.

American exceptionalism started centuries ago when talented ancestors, braving the odds, went down to the docks and climbed on ships to cross an ocean. Most people feel safer when the floor beneath their feet doesn't move.

For my grandmother, Mary Rosamilia, who arrived in New Jersy from Avellino Italy in 1901, it was the *first time she had seen a ship,* and the last time she was on one. The demands of an ocean journey filter out the timid, explaining a great deal about the American personality. We prize courage and audacity!

An equally important and related part of what contributes to America's good fortune is being located on a continent with an abundance of navigable rivers, crossing fertile farmlands. This makes it easy and reasonable to get products to market. This *network* of harbors, protected bays, navigable rivers, great lakes and canals is so widespread in the United States that most people don't realize how rare that is in the rest of the world.

The African Continent and China both have just one navigable river leading to a port. Mexico also has only one navigable river and port. The United States has more great ports fed by navigable river systems than most of the world has put together. Of course, having oceans on each side makes getting here harder, but at least once you arrive there are plenty of choices of good harbors to dock your ship.

The economic power that Northern Europe has wielded for so long comes from a *similar network* of rivers crossing through fertile lands. But those same rivers were also the source of almost endless squabbles over territory because the rivers made it difficult to protect their borders. Germany is the perfect example. They have two wonderful rivers running through their country, but it made them accessible to the armies of their neighbors, so they suffered numerous invasions. The result was that the German people became tremendously unified and organized in order to protect their sovereignty.

In contrast, the USA is *buffered* from the world by two oceans and blessed with friendly neighbors to the north and south. The Mississippi and Missouri Rivers travel from the heartland to the Gulf and both coasts have numerous great bays. New York City sits at the outlet of the great Hudson River and Philadelphia on the banks of the mighty Delaware. These two economic centers are connected by the East Coast's *intercoastal waterway*, a combination of natural and constructed passages stretching three thousand miles from Massachusetts to Texas.

It allows ships to move cargo long distances safely without having to always brave the open sea. Through incredible industry, canals have connected rivers to the Great Lakes, which themselves are a major navigation resource. Where I grew up in New Jersey, which has a remarkable industrial history, there are old *canals* from the early 1800's crisscrossing the state, connecting the rivers together with the farms and manufacturing centers.

Napa is the extreme version of that combination of those two factors: distance and accessibility. No matter which of the traditional population centers you started from, whether by land or sea, reaching Napa required a long, arduous journey and a significant amount of bravery, or foolishness. From a European point of view, Napa was the *'ends of the Earth,'* originally requiring a journey by ship around the tip of south America. Later a traveler could also choose to take the shorter route that required crossing the malarial jungle of Panama, with its torrential rain and cloying humidity on foot. The Spanish called the path that they established to connect the Atlantic to the Pacific 'El Camino Real, the Royal Road', a name they would give to the path that connected the twenty-one Franciscan Missions in California. At the time when the Canal was being constructed, there were still sections of the ancient trail visible alongside the railroad that was built to support that grand construction project.

The opening of the Panama Canal in 1914 was a *monumental* event for the Bay Area. It was celebrated the next year in San Francisco with the Panama Pacific International Exposition, a world's fair that covered a square mile of what is today the city's Marina District. It included contributions from twenty-four countries, and it dramatically showed the world that *'Frisco'* had recovered from the devastating 1906 Earthquake and fires.

The city of Napa sits at the junction of a tremendously fertile valley, and the farthest northern deep-water spot on a navigable river that empties into the San Francisco Bay. From there, ships could reach the entire Bay Area or go through the Golden Gate Pass to the Pacific Ocean and the world beyond. Only a truly adventurous seafarer would find their way up this winding river into this beautiful valley. That is why many of the earliest investors in the valley were *sea captains*. That fact set a theme for attracting brave people, with a worldly view, willing to take a chance.

When you walk up Main Street from First Street, painted on a wall is one of the wonderful murals that talk about the history of Napa. This one, just a block from the river, celebrates the docks, ships and businesses that served this area. But there are many reminders of Napa's seagoing past in the layout of the town and the buildings left behind. *Division Street,* only three and half blocks long, unaligned with the surrounding city's streets, owes its odd angle to its history as a way station where wagons lined up waiting to deliver their products to the river boats.

When you walk around the tree lined streets of 'Old Town' you'll see numerous homes sporting charming railings, banisters and decorative ship's wheels. These are all reminders of the sailing ships that brought those 'old salts' to their final port in Napa. You can always spot the oldest homes because their 'first floor' sat high above the ground to protect the living spaces from the *floods* that often occurred.

On both sides of the river are imposing stone buildings that once served the commercial docks. On the west bank is the Hatt Building that has passed through the hands of several families, and today is the home of the Napa River Inn, several stores, and charming restaurants that enjoy views of the river. If you wait long enough, you'll hear the whistle of the Napa Wine Train as it leaves its rail yard on the far bank.

In the mid 1800's San Franciscans could take a ferry to the city of Vallejo, south of Napa. There they could board the train that would take them north to downtown

Napa, or all the way up the valley to the healing waters of Calistoga.

Just a few steps farther south from the site of the old docks, was a multi-story house of ill repute, which survived from the early shipping days, up until the end of the Second World War. Seventeen miles down the Napa River in Vallejo is Mare Island. This was the Navy's first West Coast base started in 1854. During the war it was one of the busiest shipyards on the planet. On the weekends the base had a ferry boat that would bring sailors to downtown Napa, probably because it was the site of the good bars and fancy ladies.

Also, Downtown Vallejo's bars were swamped with construction workers. Today, eighty years later downtown Napa is quite different. Instead of multiple bars, it's home to the *world's greatest density* of winery tasting rooms. In place of hordes of young sailors, it attracts couples looking to spend a romantic day in wine country.

The current transformation of Downtown Napa's personality has been due entirely to its relationship with the river. The city had always been prone to flooding. When the winter rains came, the Napa River and the Napa Creek would regularly burst their banks and spread out through the downtown. Between the city's founding in the 1840's and 2005 there were *catastrophic* floods over twenty times. We're not just talking about heavy rains that saw water in the streets overshooting the curbs, for which the shopkeepers always had sandbags ready. These major floods would reach the bottoms of the Stop

Signs and take days to recede. It's not surprising that the big hotel chains and restaurants wouldn't invest there. But after a dramatic flood in 2005, the city leaders convinced the Army Core of Engineers, who are responsible for waterways, to begin a decade and a half long transformation of the river. *The river doesn't flood downtown Napa anymore* and soon after work began, major hotels and new restaurants began planning for their arrival.

As they established themselves, winery owners realized that lots of their potential customers were walking those now dry streets. They looked at the numbers and realized that having a downtown tasting room was more reasonable, and profitable, than creating one at their winery. Even larger wineries, with hospitality centers in the valley, have opened tasting rooms near the restaurants and hotels.

Meanwhile in the valley, most of the wineries now require appointments and their tasting fees have dramatically increased. So, downtown Napa has become the favorite alternative for Bay Area folks wanting to come to wine country for the day. They can stroll the sunny streets, visit the many shops, enjoy a tasting, or two, then have some lunch before they head back to the cool fog of San Francisco. That all happened when they negotiated a truce with the river!

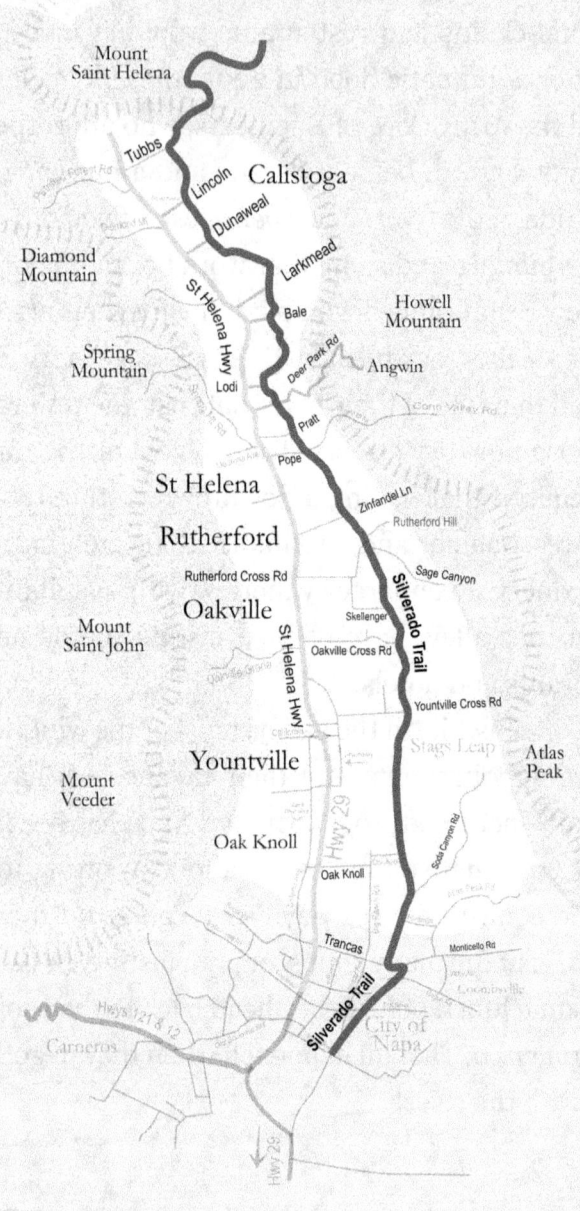

Chapter Two
The Romance of the Silverado Trail

The Silverado Trail is the quintessential California road that travels along the eastern side of the Napa Valley at the foot of the Vaca Mountains. It started as a native trail that wound its way through the hills to get above the winter flooding on the valley floor. It was made into a road by western settlers in the 1860s, to provide a winter alternative when the main road that goes up the center of the valley, Saint Helena Highway, *washed* out in the seasonal rains. But for centuries before that, the trail served a key role in the tribal economies.

Traces of the original native trail can still be found at the top of the valley within sight of Mount Saint Helena. From there it would have been a two day walk south to where the Napa River and the Napa Creek merge.

Yes, they are both named 'Napa,' and they meet right where the city of Napa was founded in 1850. south of there the river gets dramatically deeper and straighter. The Onasai, who the Spanish called the Wappo for fierce, lived in the upper valley. In the south were the Patwin, whose lands stretched along the edge of the bay and across the southern hills to the east. The Onasai would *make a deal* with the Patwin to use their 'sákas' or reed boats. From there the Onasai would have an easy, three-hour paddle south to the Sacramento River.

At that junction, just before the joined rivers empty into the great bay, there was a tribe called the 'Carquinez' whose name meant the traders. Today the bridge that spans those narrows is named for them. From there the Onasai could travel to the east on the Sacramento, or west into the bay and the world beyond. What did the Onasai have to trade? Power and efficiency, in the form of razor-sharp obsidian weapons and tools!

The Napa Valley was only shared by two human tribes, and *a formidable tribe of grizzly bears*. The upper valley, as far south as modern Yountville, was controlled by the very insular 'Onosai,' meaning the 'Outspoken Ones.' They had spread south from the lake region in order to gain control of the black volcanic glass deposits at the northeastern part of the trail. Today, that area is called Glass Mountain.

This 'glass' is actually volcanic obsidian formed millions of years ago when silica rich lava ejected from Mount Saint Helena plunged into cold lakes, instantly fusing and producing a fractured glass that is both strong and incredibly sharp. The Onosai depended on the trail and the river to trade knives, arrowheads, hatchets, and scraping tools that they fashioned from the obsidian chips.

Remnants of their handiwork have been found as far south as modern Los Angeles and as far east as Utah. The local tribes called that vital convergence of the waters where they could easily launch their boats the 'fairy village.' It seems a strange name, until you realize that ancient traditions teach that spirits and ghosts prefer to reside close to running water. This was the northern edge of the area controlled by the more populous Patwin tribe, whose villages spread all the way east into today's Solano County. Because that junction of river and creek flooded so dependably, no tribe would make a permanent encampment there, but it made a wonderful place to trade and launch their sákas.

When the Americans came, this was the location where they could sail their ships, so they built docks and warehouses there, and eventually a sprawling town. The fertility and abundance of the valley attracted sailing ships, bringing supplies and looking for local products to trade in distant markets. Many of Napa Valley's most historic wineries were built in the 1800's by wealthy ship Captains.

There are two stories behind the trail's distinctive name. The first starts with the *gold rush* in the Sierra Madre Mountains, a five-day wagon ride to the east. It attracted so many hopeful prospectors from around the world, that sailing ships arriving in San Francisco's harbor were often *stranded* there, when the crews abandoned them and headed for the hills. But refining gold requires mercury to capture the grains that are mixed with the sand. So, when that liquid metal was discovered around the hot springs that are found throughout the Napa Valley, that provided a new opportunity for the miners, and they needed a way to get there.

'Helena' as she is known locally, is just under five thousand feet tall. She's a pretty mountain with an elegant volcanic cone, that sees a frosting of snow every five years or so. When she erupted three million years ago, along with a string of other smaller mountains in Napa and Sonoma, they shaped this area's distinctive look and geology. The mercury miners, who were a particularly 'loony lot' due to their exposure to that metallic neurotoxin, named the trail after mercury's traditional title, *quicksilver*.

So, today's Silverado Trail was originally named for the Roman God, Mercury, the patron of healers and writers. Not so many years later, silver was discovered on Mount Saint Helena and the name 'Silverado Trail' remained perfectly appropriate and helpful to miners looking for work. When you stand on the slopes of the Mayacamas Mountains opposite Mount Saint Helena you can still spot the old mine's tailings, those mounded piles left behind on the graceful slopes.

As the traffic up valley increased, the locals improved the trail. Gradually its path moved to the west, closer to the edge of the valley floor. There are still parts that overlay the original, single person wide path, where countless pairs of feet carried food, supplies and obsidian tools to trade. In the upper part of the valley, you can see spots where the *steel lined wagon wheels wore grooves into the volcanic rock* that makes up those hillsides.

Today the 'Trail' is not as well-known as Saint Helena Highway, called Highway 29 by the locals. That road travels along the wide, flat valley floor, with its rich, deep soil. The Silverado Trail instead skirts the rocky, steep benchlands formed by the volcanic ridges that line the eastern edge of the valley. When the railroad tracks were laid to bring tourists to Calistoga's healing hot springs, they were run alongside Saint Helena Highway. So, while the 'Trail' was locally helpful, it wasn't widely known, until some small fame came to it thanks to a Scottish author.

Robert Louis Stevenson was *very much in love with* Fanny Van de Grift, an American magazine writer he met in Europe. Although there was a spark, she resisted his proposal for marriage, due to his malnourished, pale appearance, love of drink, uncertain income, and the fact that she was already married, with a child. She left him and England's wet climate behind and booked passage on a sailing ship home to New York, and then across the continent to her home in California. Fanny arrived safely but sickly from the arduous journey.

Robert, however, was a poet in love, so he followed her. He arrived in San Francisco in an equally pitiful state, with no guarantee that Fanny had not reconciled with her husband, or found a new handsome, healthy golden haired, California lover. Fortunately for

RLS, Fanny had not replaced him in her heart, and she opened her loving arms to his renewed marriage proposal. Why wouldn't she? Louis, as he was known among his friends, had left everything behind, crossed oceans and traveled halfway around the world to find her, he was obviously committed, and very much in love!

They had to wait for her divorce to be finalized in order to marry and then they spent the first few nights of their wedded bliss in San Francisco's famous *Palace Hotel*. Their friends, taking into consideration the newlyweds' sickly appearance, suggested that they honeymoon at the *healing spas* of Napa. The hot springs had become famous for their ability to restore health, along with the beautiful scenery, bountiful fresh food and 'good air.'

They stayed at a hotel in Saint Helena and found the climate kind, the air and food wonderful and the sunlight luminous. So, they searched for a way to extend their stay that would not use up their limited funds.

One of the locals pointed the young couple towards an abandoned mining camp on the flanks of Mount Saint Helena, where they found a two-story cabin that they *squatted* in for a two-month long honeymoon. As they gradually regained their vitality in this new Eden, Robert and Fanny were impressed so much by Napa that not surprisingly, the location found its way into his writings.

In his most famous book, 'Treasure Island,' the location of 'Lookout Mountain' was based on Mount Saint Helena, where they made their first home together, and there was more! During their sojourn they traveled throughout the valley, including visits to the Petrified Forest on top of the Mayacamas Mountains and the nearby Schramsberg Winery. They were thoroughly impressed by the wineries wonderful location, the beautiful buildings, the barrel caves dug by Chinese miners and their generous host's excellent wines.

Robert and Fanny must have been amazed by the Schram's success. Here was Jacob, a German immigrant barber, married to Annie, a local German American girl, who together made a farmstead out of a heavily wooded, up valley hillside that they turned into their own paradise.

The Stevensons' story was contained in a travelog that Robert wrote called the 'Silverado Squatters' about their home on the mountain. It contains the often-quoted phrase, for which Napa marketing folks have been eternally grateful, "Wine is bottled poetry."

But how did these young folks, with limited money, get around the valley in the 1880's? At that time, people either walked, rented horses or a wagon. They might also rely on the flexibility and generosity of the local stagecoach drivers, colorful characters, who traveled along both the Saint Helena Highway and the Silverado Trail!

Luckily, they were befriended by a man called 'John Silverado' because he ran the Silverado Trail stagecoach line. He was a very tall, commanding gent who towered over most other folks, earning him the popular moniker 'Long John.' As any reader of the great adventure novel 'Treasure Island' knows, the swashbuckling, peg-legged pirate at the heart of that story is named Long John Silver! I have often wondered if that flamboyant wagon driver, a predecessor of the local tour guides, who are themselves a colorful group, happened to wear a patch over one eye? Argh!

Chapter Three
Who Named Mount Saint Helena?

One of my favorite stories, because it's both adventurous and romantic, is how Mount Saint Helena got her name. This very pretty mountain towers over the northern end of the Napa Valley, standing just under five thousand feet tall, and looking like *the volcanic cone that she was three million years ago.* Many new visitors to the West Coast, when they first hear the name, confuse this with Mount Saint Helens, the volcano in Washington State that famously erupted in 1980.

People are horrible at geography! Saint Helena, in comparison, is about three thousand feet smaller. She's more of a 'designer mountain,' good looking, graceful and accessible.

She does have warm feet, because thermal tubes from more recent volcanos to the north pass under her skirts. Those tubes provide the heat for the popular hot springs that boil to the surface in the town of Calistoga. Sam Brannan, who founded the town in the mid-1800's, claimed it would be the "Saratoga Springs of California." Sam inadvertently named the town when, during a brandy-soaked event for his investors at his hot springs spa, his inebriated tongue claimed it would be "The Calistoga of Sarafornia!" Of course, in a town with such a good sense of humor, there is a *Café Sarafornia*.

While Mount Saint Helena looks like a volcanic cone from the Napa Valley floor, when you see her from Northern Sonoma, sailing over the ridges of the Mayacamas mountain range that separates the two counties, she appears as a rambling series of descending mounds *in the shape of a woman's body*. That distinctive shape is part of one of the stories behind the naming of the mountain. This is the quintessential example of a wine country story because there are at least four versions that all sound mostly feasible. Which story you hear depends on where you are and who is telling it, and how much wine has been consumed.

Not surprisingly, you'll hear different versions of the story in Napa and Sonoma. In Napa, the story goes that the mountain was named by a Russian Princess who climbed the mountain in the 1800's. Many people don't realize that while Northern California was the northern tip of the Spanish empire, it was also the southern tip of the Russian Empire's reach in the Americas. The icy

Russian seal hunting camps in Alaska needed provisions and they saw the temperate Sonoma coast as the solution. Princess Elena, her husband and three children were in the party that traveled in two ships to Sonoma where they established a farming community. Compared to frozen Alaska, this slice of the coast was a little piece of heaven, where the fields for grazing livestock stayed green most of the year, and everything they planted quickly sprouted and prospered.

The locals called it Fort Ross, or 'Rooss,' or 'Rossiya', for Mother Russia. Considering *the diverse languages spoken in the area; Spanish, English, Russian, Polish, Chinese, Kodiak, Pomo, Patwin and Onasai,* it's amazing that the name stayed that close to the original. While that explains how the Russian River Valley got its name, it still seems strange that a Princess would find herself on the far ends of the Earth and have the opportunity to name a mountain.

The story I heard was that the Princess Elena Pavlovna Gagarina, *the niece of the Czarina and an exceptionally beautiful young woman, fell in love with a handsome Count.* He was brave, resourceful and a renowned poet. But Alexander Rotchev's rank was many steps below that of his beloved Elena. In the Russian Court rank mattered, so not surprisingly, the Czarina did not give her blessing for the marriage. Elena followed her heart and they married anyway. Amazingly, the Count's opportunities dried up. After a long wait, he was offered a posting at the camp in Alaska, the farthest and coldest reaches of the Russian Empire. Here's an important lesson, when someone holds your fate in their hands, don't piss off the Czarina! So, the Count bundled his wife and their young children, off to the ends of the Earth.

Fortunately for the young couple, the governor of Alaska saw Alexander as a man he could trust to accomplish a difficult venture. He also probably felt sorry for this sophisticated, young family struggling in the frozen wasteland. So, he assigned Alexander to take those two ships, and his family, and sail south along the coast to establish a farming community.

It had to be done carefully because the British had claimed the coast of Canada. Further south, New England sea captains held sway over what is today Washington and Oregon and dominated shipping along the Pacific Coast. They originally ventured there to hunt whales, but then found a profitable living transporting finished products from the New England workshops and factories to the settlers and gold miners.

On Spain Street in downtown Sonoma is a pretty, Victorian house that is home to a restaurant called the General's Daughter. It was built in New England and transported in pieces in the belly of a sailing ship for General Vallejo as a wedding gift for one of his daughters. His own house, built in the same New England workshops, is a short walk away. It sits below the 'Lachryma Montis' springs, the 'tears of the mountain.' That was also the name of Vallejo's wine brand when he was one of the biggest producers in the North Bay.

The Russians couldn't travel far south without upsetting the Spanish Governor, who resided in

Monterey, and who had a small garrison on the San Francisco Bay. The Spanish considered 'Alta California', as it was known, a wild place. Their settlements there probably only developed due to the spice trade. The Galleons, returning from the Philippines rode the circular Pacific currents. Their first landfall was normally along the Northern California coast. As they made their way south at about six knots, they explored the coast looking for bays where they could moor and take on fresh water and provisions. One of the first bays they discovered was Carmel and that became the home of the first Northern California Franciscan Mission.

So as Alexander and Elena sailed south, they had to find a spot that the English, Americans and Spaniards were not interested in. They settled on a piece of the California coast just north of the Russian River delta. While the river is too shallow for a ship, it was perfect for the sturdy Aleut hunters and their kayaks, which they brought along on their incessant search for furs. To say this spot, covered with towering redwood forests, was remote is an understatement. It was the middle of nowhere! Even today, with good roads and driving in a car it's a hike!

Because Northern California was so difficult to reach, it was a land of brave and capable adventurers, and its fair share of fools. Imagine the splash it created to have this brilliant and sophisticated couple arrive in their midst. That Elena was a true blonde beauty, certainly turned many heads in this land that was populated by dark haired Spaniards and native tribes. Despite the Fort's remote location, the Princess and the Count hosted local dignitaries including General Vallejo and his ally, Chief Solano.

They in turn were welcomed at the General's home in Sonoma. The fact that Mariano Guadalupe Vallejo had been sent north to keep the Russians from expanding their operations to the south seems to have been temporarily forgotten. That is not surprising. *This charming couple, who were so obviously in love,* brought some very appreciated glamour and sophistication to this rustic place. From Mariano's point of view, they were a wonderful addition, and Mexico City was very far away.

Princess Elena and her husband Alexander were the last directors of Russia's settlement in California. Well before the Czar's final days, seventy years later, they abandoned it because of increasing pressure from the Americans who were flooding the area. Here we get to the first two stories about the naming of Mount Saint Helena. Before they left, Elena, or 'Helena' took the opportunity to travel throughout the area with two Russian scientists who were recording their observations of the area. Of course, they brought along some hardy helpers with rifles because this area had a lively community of fierce braves and California Grizzly Bears.

From Sonoma they could see Mount Mayacamas, as the natives called Mount Saint Helena, towering over the mountain ridge to the east. Elena, with the scientists and bodyguards, trekked over the hills and climbed the almost 5,000-foot peak. She was clearly a very vigorous woman because it's quite a climb. The name was changed from Mayacamas, which meant 'many springs,' when the climbing party installed a bronze plaque at the peak declaring it to be Mount Saint Helena and including the names of various Russian dignitaries.

The name Elena is a variation of Helena, Ilona and Helen. In Napa, the story goes that it was named for Princess Elena. The second variation was that Princess Elena named it for the Czarina's patron Saint, 'Helena,' the mother of the Roman Emperor Constantine, who was the Pontifex Maximus of the Roman Church and coincidentally a famous Astrologer. It was Mama Helena who convinced her son to make Christianity the Empire's official religion. *As the mother of Russia, it was natural that Czarina Alexandra's patron Saint* would be the Emperor's mother who changed the Christian world.

One could imagine that Princess Elena, a sophisticated young woman *banished to the far reaches of the Earth,* wanted to get back in the Czarina's good graces, and return to the comforts of the royal court. We can also imagine her writing the Czarina a letter in her beautiful Cyrillic hand, "Dear Auntie Alexandra, I've named a beautiful mountain for your favorite Saint, can I come home now, please?" and then sealing the letter with wax, a prayer and a tear.

It was not long after the naming of the mountain that the Russians gave up their 'Fort' on the Sonoma coast. Did she and her husband return home to the Russian Court, or did they make their way in California? No one seems to know. Hopefully, their future was as interesting as their past.

There is a second, more romantic version of this story. In that one, Count Alexander and a party of scientists climbed the mountain and installed the plaque. The Helena he was thinking about was his beloved wife Elena, the mother of his children, who had followed him to the ends of the Earth for love.

Now, if you are in Sonoma, the naming of Mount Saint Helena is a different tale. When you see the mountain from the Santa Rosa plains, it's even more impressive than the solitary cone you see from southern Napa. In Sonoma it becomes a long, rambling mountain ridge. In an area where the hills stand between 1,000 and 2,000 feet, Mount Saint Helena, at just under 5000 feet can be seen for many miles around. I heard this story of the naming of Mount Saint Helena from an archaeologist at Fort Ross, so I would normally give it a bit more credence than I give to other wine country stories I've heard.

That's because the stories you hear in Wine Country often benefit from artistic additions, inspired by both the storyteller and the audience being under the influence of some wonderful wines. Our stories are a perfect example of that! With that said, there are some other factors that cast some doubt on this source for the name.

According to my friend at Fort Ross, the mountain was already called Mount Saint Helena before Elena, or Alexander climbed the mountain with their plaque. In this story, the Mountain was first named by the Franciscan missionary, Altamira, who saw it from, what is today, Santa Rosa, which has the distinction of being the Northern most major California city with a Spanish name.

Naming every place after Saints, or Angels was normal. Santa Rosa gets its name from 'Saint Rose of Lima,' the first Saint of the Americas.

The story goes that the shape of Saint Helena, which resembles a reclining woman, reminded Altamira of a funerary statue in a church in France. The Patron Saint of the church was Saint Helena. While being named by one of the Franciscan missionaries is always historically notable, this particular Franciscan's history in Northern California is so checkered and vainglorious that it makes you wonder, whether his story about naming the mountain was true.

We know that he established the Sonoma Mission at Los Carneros, close to the bay, *because he was very wary of the tribes to the north* that he would encounter on the way to Santa Rosa.

While the Governor in Monterey had given him soldiers to help, it was a small contingent and Altamira was famously unpopular with the local tribes. In any case, what are the chances that he traveled up the Sonoma Valley to where he could see the mountain? It is more likely that he received descriptions of the mountain from soldiers and recorded the name on a map! *But did he name it, or was he told the name and wove a good story to give himself the credit?*

Cartography is an interesting profession. Here is an interesting fact that is possibly not taught in schools anymore. The way the Americas got their name was because one of the first popular maps of the Americas was based on charts provided by Amerigo Vespucci.

He signed his name very prominently on the unexplored landmass beyond the coastline, so the mapmakers assumed that was its name. Later when they realized their mistake they changed it on later maps, depending on which countries claimed the various parts of the coast, but the name stuck. Amerigo does have the distinction of being the first person to postulate that this was an entirely different continent, and not part of Asia, as had been previously assumed.

The adventures of the Franciscan Missionaries north of the bay were short-lived. Eight years after the Sonoma Mission was established under Imperial Mexico, the Mexican Revolution happened and the leaders in Mexico City considered the church an agent of the aristocracy. Any native-born Spaniards, who had not become citizens of Mexico, were forced out and Padre Altamira was sent packing back to Barcelona and was never heard from again. The missions were secularized and the mission buildings on the Sonoma Plaza became General Vallejo's property.

Like so many Sonoma buildings on the Plaza, the San Francisco Solano Mission survived because they could not afford to replace it. Its sister Mission to the south in San Rafael was taken down when they built a very impressive Spanish style church. Years later, when a group wanted to build a re-creation of the mission building, they had no record of what it looked like. So, they built it using an image found on a popular set of postcards. One slight problem! The publishing company didn't know what the building looked like either.

So, they substituted a different view of the very pretty Carmel mission, which had survived nicely.

One More Story

Now those are the first three stories about the naming of Mount Saint Helena, and I promised you four. While you can see Saint Helena from Sonoma, she is very much Napa's Mountain. The town of Napa was founded at the northernmost point that can be reached with a sailing ship so many of Napa's earliest investors were sea captains. The Mexicans didn't prefer Napa for two reasons. First, it's much drier than Sonoma, and second, it was inhabited by the fierce Onasai/Wappo tribe and a multitude of giant California Grizzly bears. *It was much safer to stay in Sonoma!*

But many of the Americans who settled in Napa were sailors, soldiers, military men, mountain men and wagon train leaders. They were adventurous and accustomed to dealing with trouble.

To provide a little context, let's mention that when California became part of the United States, the Presidio at Sonoma became the central Fort for Northern California. Many of the famous Civil War Generals visited the area and the famous General Hooker, whose exploits are well recorded, lived in Sonoma for many years. Today there is a nearby creek named for him and his home, which is just off the Sonoma Plaza, serves as the local Historical Society. There is an old story that the term "Hooker" comes from the numerous 'loose women' that frequented his headquarters. Ever since his service in the Mexican American war there were always ladies around who admired the 'Handsome General." *As the Army moved from camp to camp, they became known as Hooker's Girls.* While the term hooker did appear in print in the years before the General came to prominence, his tendency to run a camp that other officers described as part bar and part brothel, surely helped to make the term more popular.

But back to the story! In Napa, it was the ship captains who left their mark, and their homes, alongside the river. With many of them being New Englanders, they favored Victorian-style homes, but with a California flair. As word of Napa's beautiful, fertile valley and easy access to the bay spread among the sea going community, it attracted more sailors. One of them was *a sea captain from England. He arrived with a purse full of money after a successful trip* and went looking for land in Napa. An adventurous soul looking for a good deal, the captain looked in the far north end of the valley, finally buying a large piece of land that included Mount Saint Helena.

As he stood atop this grand mountain and looked out over the beautiful valley, he realized it was his mountain to name. So, he named it after the ship that had brought him to San Francisco and provided the wealth he needed to make a home in this American Eden. The name of that ship was the 'Saint Helena.' Was it just a coincidence? Did he arrive and find that the mountain had the same name as his ship? Sailors are a superstitious lot, and he could have taken that as a lucky sign! Of course, with time and enough good bottles of wine and brandy, the story more than likely evolved until it was the Captain that coined the name for his pretty little mountain, sitting at the top of a gorgeous valley, north of the San Francisco Bay.

I am not sure which of these stories is true, although *I expect that there's some truth here and there, in bits and pieces.* The one thing that I do know is true and obvious, Mount Saint Helena knew what she wanted to be called.

Chapter Four
Napa's Great Buildings

Wine Country has a wonderful collection of winery buildings. The first were built in the early 1800s, and many of those are still in use today. The builders began by using redwood, either found on the site, or brought from the towering forests that blanket the Pacific Coast. Even though those beautiful, red boards stand up well to bugs and rot, they are not as durable as stone. So, in the late 1800's the builders turned to masonry, which has long been considered the ideal material for a winery.

Stone is perfect for a building which needs to stay cool and humid while standing up to water and the acids found in wine. Starting in the 1970's there was an influx of international companies building dramatic wineries where the architecture would add to the attraction.

But when the Spanish first arrived in the North Bay, they just needed to make wine.

The region's first prominent winemaker was a native '*Californio*' and Spanish officer, General Mariano Guadalupe Vallejo, born in Monterey on July 4th, a date of which he was particularly proud due its affinity with the United States. Mariano produced wine under his label, 'Lachryma Montis,' or *'the Tears of the Mountain,'* named for the spring above his home in Sonoma.

It was from his vineyards that *George Yount, mountain man and wagon train leader,* purchased the first grape vines planted in the heart of the Napa Valley. Yount's Caymus Spring Ranch was a grant from General Vallejo.

Those early winemakers planted high sugar Mission grapes and fermented them in tanks made from cow hides hung on a frame. But they soon learned from the winemakers who came there from Hungary, Prussia, France and Italy, who were well aware of the advantages that wooden tanks and stone buildings provided to the winemaker.

Fortunately for the Napa winemakers, when they wanted to build their wineries in the late 1800's, Sonoma was awash in Italian immigrants, a culture with an ancient masonry tradition. Because Sonoma is so similar to Piedmont, Italy, boatloads of young Italian men came there looking for work.

At that time the cheapest berth on a steamer was equivalent to a long-distance bus ticket today. Italy is a mountainous country blessed with abundant quarries of marble, granite, and alabaster, so the profession of mason is more common than that of carpenter. In Italy a wood parquet floor is considered a greater luxury than the more common marble.

Wine Country was not the only beneficiary of this migratory event. The wonderful stone buildings that grace our *Ivy League Universities* were built by Italian masons, whose descendants often still live in those towns. Most of America's stone churches and the most ornate of Washington DC's government buildings owe their stately beauty to those anonymous Italian stone masons and sculptors.

No matter how much an architect tries to impose their design style on a building, the people who use their hands to build it always get a vote. In downtown Napa the Italian craftsmen's influence on a very non-Italian building, is there for everyone to see. The historic Presbyterian Church on Third and Randolph was built in 1889. Traditionally, American Presbyterian churches are simpler than the elaborate Catholic Churches.

Yet this towering wooden building is dramatic, with its big stained-glass windows, and most notably, numerous figures adorning the outside, very much in the Roman Catholic style. Why? Because Italian craftsmen built it, and in their eyes, a church *needed statues of the Saints* adorning the exterior to welcome the congregation. More than likely the supervising architect was busy with another project, and by the time he came back the workers were putting away their tools and heading to another job site. Any changes cost extra!

Successful buildings need to stand up to the prevailing weather, even in California's lovely Mediterranean climate that is so kind to humans, grapes and olives. Visitors from colder climes are often surprised to hear that the mountaintops lining the valleys get traces of snow every few winters, like *the dusting of sugar* on top of an almond croissant from our famous bakeries. The Northern Italian masons seemed to have missed that point because they built substantial structures prepared to endure hundreds of years of rain, ice and snow, even though we don't do that kind of weather here!

That does explain why these great stone structures still look so good after twelve decades, despite having endured multiple earthquakes and thirty to forty years of abandonment due to Prohibition. Admittedly the mason's propensity to overbuild was thoroughly supported by the Vermont born, and New England trained architect and winery engineer Hamden McIntyre. He had built wineries in the Finger Lakes region of New York State and worked as a marine engineer in Canada and Alaska.

When the first stone wineries were being imagined McIntyre was working in San Francisco. He had come to California to help re-organize a newly formed shipping partnership, Hansen, Nybom and Company.

The youngest partner, whom *Hamden* befriended, was *Captain Gustave Niebaum*, a Finnish American ship captain who made a fortune shipping furs from Alaska. Gustave eventually changed the Finnish spelling of his name Nybom, to the German spelling in deference to his German Jewish partners.

As Niebaum grew increasingly wealthy, he dreamed of outfitting a ship and sailing the world with his beloved German American wife, and then buying a French Chateau. But Suzanne, born in California, didn't like boats, hated the ocean and didn't want to live in France, so far from her home. Instead, they decided to build Napa's first grand winery, naming it Inglenook, which they call a small, cozy seating nook, big enough for two, alongside a fireplace.

They built a Victorian mansion at the foot of the Mayacamas mountains in Rutherford, *with a carriage house where the captain made his first wine.* Gustave traveled throughout Europe as far east as Hungry, to observe wine making techniques. He brought back a wide variety of grape vines he planted in their vineyards, including many that are popular today. While Gustave and Suzanne Niebaum never had children, they adopted his wife's niece and nephew and raised them as their own.

In an interesting case of history repeating itself, many years later when the Coppola's bought the house. *Francis made his first wine in that same carriage house and called it Rubicon.* As you might recall from Roman history, the Rubicon River was the northern border between Gaul and Italy. When Julius Caesar came back from his triumphant five years in what is today's modern France, his enemies in the Senate planned to ruin him in the courts. To save his honor he led a small portion of his army across the river, the official border of Italy, which made him a rebel. His famous quote as they road into the water was, *"Let the dice fly high."*

His enemies were so terrified by his approach that they abandoned the city, and the treasury stuffed with gold and he because the virtual ruler of Rome. By naming the wine Rubicon, they were saying that now that they made their first wine, there was no turning back.

But back to Niebaum's marvelous building. The captain wanted to build a state-of-the-art winery in Napa, thousands of miles from France so he engaged an architect who understood the aesthetics of a classic building. But he was not familiar with gravity fed wineries. Fortunately, McIntyre had been trained in winemaking and knew all about wineries, so he came on as the project's general manager.

That's not to say that the Captain wasn't deeply involved in creating the winery. *His agents throughout Europe continued to send him books* on the latest advances in winemaking methods and technology, and these were incorporated into the building and winery processing.

The Inglenook Winery design was such a success that Hamden McIntyre spent many years designing some of Napa's most famous winery buildings. Considering that Hamden's original training included wooden New England style buildings, it's said that only two of his local redwood wineries remain. The first is the winemaking barn at Frog's Leap in Rutherford, with its jaunty leaping frog weathervane. *Their slogan is, "Time's fun when you're having flies."* The other is the classic, three story Eschol winery, today owned by the Trefethen family, at the corner of Saint Helena Highway and Oak Knoll, surrounded by their five-hundred-acre vineyard.

The story goes that it was McIntyre's favorite and that his ghost haunts it. However, that's pretty unlikely. Not that it's haunted, wine country has plenty of ghosts. But it's not McIntyre, because even though he was in high demand for his winery designs, Hamden and Susan moved back to Vermont where he stayed productive, although not building his wonderful wineries.

If you love buildings, please visit the Trefethen winery, because it is a wonderful example of the New England woodworker's art with its massive beams and classic joints. Another example is the red barn at the Nickel and Nickel property in Oakville. Built in the 1700's, *it was disassembled and transported to the estate where it was carefully reassembled.*

I've walked though many of these classic barns and I thought I knew a bit about them, but then the director of Napa's Historical Society filled in a fascinating connection. The wood joints that hold the classic New England barns together *are the same designs as those used on sailing ships of the period.* How did that happen? Simple, the same craftsman built both barns and ships, moving back and forth between the country and the coast with the seasons.

This combination of well-traveled European investors, sturdy northern Italian stonemasons and a New England winery engineer resulted in a collection of wineries that often resemble fortresses, like Far Niente,

Chateau Montelena, Greystone and many more. These grand structures are interspersed with dozens of smaller stone buildings from that period. This was the *last great expression* of the traditional builders' art that had developed over the centuries. As the twentieth century dawned, natural stone was eclipsed by steel, aluminum, plywood and sheet rock.

In 1919 Prohibition began and most of the winery buildings were abandoned. Even though it ended thirteen years later, many growers had shifted to other crops. It wasn't until the 1970s, when there were more orchards than vineyards in the valley, that the interest in growing premium wine grapes locally was revived. That's when investors began looking at these great structures and imagining the possibilities.

One of the hidden advantages that often made the expense of renovation worthwhile was an idiosyncrasy of the winery regulations. It's much easier legally to establish a new winery on a site where a previous one had operated, even if just one corner of that building remains.

When building in California, one must always consider the effects of *earthquakes*, because they will eventually happen! One of the more interesting stories I heard is about our dear Inglenook. After the devastating 6.9 Loma Prieta earthquake, that shook the 1989 World Series, engineers examined public buildings to determine how to make them safe. They were followed by tradesmen with bolts, straps and steel to stop structures from being knocked off their foundations, or crumbling.

The main building at Inglenook is an impressive pile of stone quarried from the property, along with a significant amount poured concrete. It is three stories tall, sitting on thick walls, cut by narrow windows, with a series of arched chambers on the first floor to store wine barrels.

As is common with gravity fed wineries like Far Niente and Graystone, Inglenook is built into a hillside. That allowed grape wagons to drive up the low hill behind the winery to the level of the very solid second floor. There men would unload bins of grapes into the fermentation tanks. Finally, when the yeast had turned the juice into wine, a hose was attached to the tank and run down to the first floor. They would open the valve and fill the empty aging barrels without needing a pump. This was important in the days before electric and pneumatic pumps were commonplace. In those days moving juice required either a siphon and buckets, or a manual pump with a long handle and a *strong arm*.

Because Inglenook's concrete second story was so substantial, McIntyre knew it made the upper building heavy, so he planned for that. The masons embedded old trolley car cables into the wet concrete of that thick, second floor. The ends were *anchored into the hillside*, to prevent the earthquakes, that would surely come from breaking up Inglenook's tight embrace of its hillside. Today, the building and grounds enjoy an abundance of care and it's surely worth the visit. As the engineers inspected the building, they were amazed that it didn't suffer any structural damage in the quake."

A *horrible* example of what a quake can do was Trefethen's wooden winery. The 2014 Napa quake happened during harvest, and even though the wooden building no longer operates as a gravity fed winery, they had wine barrels, filled with water, on the second floor preparing to accept new wine. It made the building top heavy enough to magnify the quake's effects.

The result that I saw driving up the valley was a building leaning over about four feet. Those huge one hundred-and twenty-year-old redwood beams had bent but not broken. That great building never let go of its foundation.

When they started the restoration, they attached cables to the upright beams and anchored them to the foundation at the back of the building. They planned to do a *'chiropractic adjustment,'* cranking the cables tighter and tighter until the building stood straight. They were hoping to get an inch of movement a day, but on the first day those big beams flexed, and the building stood right up, within inches of its original position. After the family's herculean efforts, it is still greeting visitors today.

The Far Niente Winery was built at the same time and also into a small knoll, with two driveways running up the hill to the two upper floors. Today, when you visit the winery, the very top floor is a charming reception area, with a long table for guests and windows that look east over the vineyards. The building was the work of the Italian masons who carved the words *'Far Niente'* into the lintel above the planned cave entrance, that were dug almost ninety years later. Those words are a fragment of the winery's original name, 'In Dolce Far Niente,' which itself is a shortened version of the original Italian expression, "Il dolce piacere per far niente," meaning *'the sweet pleasure of doing nothing.'*

For men who worked daily with blocks of stone, hammers, chisels and hand cranked cranes, their leisure time must have been especially sweet. The building sat empty for many years, but not entirely due to prohibition.

During that unfortunate period when making wine was illegal, a wealthy widow lived in the home with her young and dashing second husband, who had been a World War One flying Ace. He built an *airstrip* on the property and routinely smuggled liquor out of the valley in his airplane. His entrepreneurial venture came to an unfortunate end when his wife's daughter, who had no affection for her stepfather, poisoned him!

After that, the joy pretty much went out of the home, and it sat empty for many years. When the current owners, the Nickel family, took it over in the 1970's they found that the structure was so well built that the main task, prior to installing the new systems, was removing the trees and bushes that had overtaken the property in the ensuing years. *Then they dug the caves.*

Not every stone building from that era was so fortunate. At the top of the valley at the northern edge of the town of Saint Helena, a very long and tall building called Greystone towers over the road. It was once the home of the Christian Brothers Cellars, but thanks to the Loma Prieta earthquake, it is now the west coast home of The Culinary Institute of America.

Unlike Inglenook and Far Niente, which were built into knolls on the settled valley floor, Greystone was built into an unstable hillside in the narrowest part of the valley. This is where the western slope of the volcanic Vaca Mountains *almost touches* the eastern slope of the Mayacamas Mountains, that in this part of the valley contains a great deal of volcanic ash. The two ranges form a mile wide neck on the bottom-heavy hourglass shape that describes the Napa Valley.

The hillside is so steep that Greystone's parking lot sits high above the road, where a long flight of steep stairs brings you up to the first floor. At the back of that ground floor, Chinese workers had dug a wine cave that went deep into the hillside. Inside the central entranceway, multiple open staircases wind their way up to the top floor where the cooking school now resides. This complex balancing act of leaning against the hill and defying gravity worked well for many years, *until* the Loma Prieta earthquake gave those ashy hillsides a serious shaking.

At the time, the Christian Brothers had been making wine there for many years and aging it in the caves below. As an aside, in case you're wondering whether these are natural caves, while in the long history of winemaking, natural caves have been employed, the caves in the north bay were, and continue to be dug by industrious miners.

After the quake, the inherent instability that existed on that hillside made itself known. It required an extensive amount of work to prevent the building's walls from heading off in different directions. This required the installation of a constellation of *'earthquake stars'* that can be seen on the front of the building. They serve as the end nuts for steel rods that span the building and connect the front and back walls together, preventing them from spreading apart.

The place where this instability was most obvious was in the dirt below, where the cave was located. It was also the place that would be the hardest and most expensive to fix, because there's an awful lot of unstable stone on top of those caves and gravity is undeniable. For the Christian Brothers this was a disaster because having a cool, humid cave to age their wine was essential.

Eventually, Christian Brothers decided to move to another facility and the building was sold to the Culinary Institute of America *for a dollar*, with the
acceptance that it was up to the new owners to do the required repairs. Fortunately, the CIA, as it's known locally, was looking for a West Coast location.

Sonoma was also in the running, but the Greystone property was a good solution for them for an odd reason. They were one of the few potential buyers in the heart of Wine Country that wasn't a winery, so they didn't care about the condition of the caves.

While the 'earthquake stars' on the exterior can be mistaken for decorations, inside the north part of the building that is less supported by the hill, there is so much structural steel arching through the rooms that you feel like you're standing inside the upper parts of the Brooklyn Bridge.

That part of the Valley, on the edge of the little town of Saint Helena, is also home to Napa's oldest winery, Charles Krug. It was started on land that was part of his wife's dowry. Charles had worked for the Count over in Sonoma as a winemaker, before he started his own winery, which he owned for a short time. But the ensuing owners built two remarkable stone buildings, one for the winery and an expansive carriage house that today is used for events.

The Mondavi family came north from the Central Valley after WWII and bought the winery and ran it as a family affair. After the famous feud between the two brothers, Robert took his share and started his own winery, and Peter's family has continued to make their wines there in a modern, solar powered building. The historic winery is used for aging barrels and hospitality. One of Krug's employees was fellow Prussian, Jacob Beringer.

While Jacob worked at Krug, his brother in New York was raising money, and eventually they bought the land across the street and started the Beringer Brothers Winery in 1876. The stone winery buildings were tucked against the hill so they could dig caves in the back. Their most remarkable architectural contribution was their Rhine House.

To build it Jacob moved a spacious, California style home to the north where it is surrounded by a lovely grove of redwood trees. This way his emblematic building would stand out prominently just inside the gate. The Rhine House was based on their childhood home in Prussia, so the fish and birds portrayed in the stained-glass windows are those breeds found *near their ancestral home.* The dining room windows include food themes, the drawing room tea and beverages.

This impressively beautiful building was one of Napa's first great 'castles'. Today the mansion that was once their home is used for pouring their most expensive wines, while the old winery building is used for the rest of the list. The wines are made across the road, outside in an orderly collection of stainless-steel tanks you can see as you drive by on Saint Helena Highway.

Another contemporary winery in that neighborhood is on the road up to Spring Mountain. It was built buy a *Monsieur Parrot,* the French son of Captain Gustave Niebaum's business partner in their wildly successful shipping company. It includes an impressive hillside cave fronted by a dramatic steeple.

He and his wife were planning their home just after Jacob Beringer had completed his dramatic Rhine House, that was turning everyone's head. For Monsieur and Madame Parrot, it was a daunting task trying to keep up with the Berringer's' love of expensive, decorative woods and stained glass, *so they took a simpler route.* Parrot simply told their architect,

> *'We don't care what it looks like so much, as long as it's taller than the Beringer's house,' and it is!*

In an interesting Hollywood twist, the house was used in the 1980's 'nighttime soap opera' Falcon Crest, about wealthy families of wine country. The intro featured the image of a falcon from one of the house's stained-glass windows. In the true spirit of Hollywood, the part of *the titular Falcon shown in the window, was played by a parrot,* the namesake of the family Parrot!

The same masons that built the wineries laid the blocks and bricks for many of the charming storefront buildings in downtown Saint Helena and Napa. Those materials set them apart from downtown Sonoma on the other side of the Mayacamas Mountains. There you'll find a wonderful collection of adobe buildings constructed during the Spanish colonial period, with their soft, rounded edges, enclosing courtyards and paseos, shielded from the heat. The main reason that Sonoma never replaced the buildings was money, there is no river nearby so there was less commerce. But, because downtown Sonoma lacked a river, they didn't suffer from Napa's devastating floods, so they simply repaired the buildings they had, including the historic Mission and the Presidio Barracks.

In comparison, the Napa River promoted so much commercial activity, and the downtown was so subject to

floods, that the owners could afford to tear down the single-story, mud adobes and replace them with more durable, multi-story stone buildings, in the early 1900's. The only historic Napa adobe was beautifully restored and today is home to a restaurant south of downtown Napa.
It was the home of the original Mexican settler and his family, Sergeant Nicolás Higuera, who had received a massive land grant from his commander, General Vallejo. His ranchero included what is today downtown Napa and a large part of Los Carneros.

    In 2014 the Napa Quake destructively shook the downtown, where massive stone blocks flew off the fronts of the turn of the century buildings. In Sonoma, even though the quake burst the wine tanks at the downtown Sebastiani winery, the historic adobes came through it with just a few cracks. Rebuilding downtown Napa was a lengthy process because those Italian stone masons are long gone, and today fewer people possess those remarkable and enduring skills.

Today the masons are still mostly immigrants, and they continue to build remarkable structures. One of the most beautiful modern wineries in Napa is Darioush. It is constructed from golden travertine marble quarried in Iran and milled and carved in Italy and Turkey. It is patterned on the ancient Persian capital *Persepolis*. I also heard that it was based on *Heliopolis*, the temple of the Sun, which seems suitable considering the material and design.

It is a beautifully balanced building, with a large complex cave underneath. The center front section is for hospitality, while the left wing is their office. The winery is at the back and separated by a glass wall. The right wing is a home. Outside at the north side of the building is an amphitheater, where the upper rows are at ground level, and the bottom is at the same level as the cave floor. The front of the building faces west, but the draining effects of the afternoon sun are mitigated by the rich colors of the materials.

As you approach Darioush columns mimic a line of trees, topped with sculptures of horses. On either side are ponds with water flowers. In the center is a sunken area with steps down to the paved floor. This is a seating area that I've only seen used once. It was filled with low, Persian cushions, and an off-white cloth was draped over the tops of the columns to provide shade, making it an amazingly appealing space.

For all the chateaus, villas and mansions that populate the North Bay, the Castello di Amorosa in Northern Napa has the greatest right to the title, *'Castle,'* because it was patterned on Tuscan Medieval castles. The person who dreamed this up was Dario Sattui, of the long-time V. Sattui Winery.

Thanks to its location in a commercial zone, instead of the restrictive Agricultural Preserve, V. Sattui is able to have a deli with picnic tables. When I started wine touring in 2005, one out of every eight Napa visitors tasted at V. Sattui and then had lunch there.

After a good run Dario was semi-retired, spending half his time in Italy. But back in Napa Valley he bought a hillside vineyard behind a large house just south of downtown Calistoga that he planned to turn into a Bed and Breakfast.

The next part of the story is a bit of my speculation about how the idea for a castle winery in Napa came about. About the time when he was living in Tuscany, a local family was building a winery styled as a castle. You could see it from the Autostrada, along with a very tall, turquoise crane.

The idea of creating a destination winery in Tuscany was quite a departure. Italy has half a million wineries and the place is practically carpeted in vineyards, so having a winery in your neighborhood is about as common as having a bakery. It must have got Dario thinking, "If they can build a castle winery in Tuscany, why can't I build one in Napa?" so he did! He had architects create plans of various Tuscan castles and then they got together and created a new design. They built an authentic hundred and seven room, eight level high stone castle, using tons of building materials, including wrought iron and carvings from Italy.

He named it Castello Di Amorosa, or 'Castle of the Beloved.' Was it a good bet? I was there two weeks after it opened, when I hadn't seen a single advertisement for it yet, and they were already *booked to capacity*. Another time I dropped by with my daughter and Disney was shooting the movie 'Bedtime Story' starring Adam Sandler.

For that they finally filled the moat with water and in return the crew built an impressive Medieval village that extended from the front path to the drawbridge and into the courtyard. But even during filming, the tasting room downstairs stayed open.

El Castello is *one of three destination wineries within sight of its parapets*. The original star of the upper valley was Sterling, opening their white, Greek, Mykonos Island style winery on the top of a hill in the 1970's. It features a tramway to carry visitors from the parking lot up to the winery with its splendid views. Sterling was the first winery to charge for tastings, although you could say that the guests paid for the tram ride, and once they arrived at the top the wines were free.

Just across the street from the entrance to Sterling is Clos Pegase. Traditionally, Clo in the name of a French winery means a walled, or enclosed vineyard. Clo Pegase was originally home to a wonderful sculpture collection, inside of a *delightfully colorful Michael Graves designed building*.

Being able to taste their wines while surrounded by this wonderful collection of art was a unique experience. Periodically they had artists in residence who would use the tank room as their studio and gallery. But things change. Clos Pegase was sold, and the art collection departed with the owner. For some unknown and ill-informed reason, the new *owners painted that beautiful, uniquely colored building a remarkably boring gray*. But it has sold again and the new owners plan to restore the orginal paint scheme.

Then, in 2020 the North Napa fire burned massive tracts above downtown Saint Helena, forcing part of the town's evacuation. The fire raged up Howell Mountain and the firebrands blew across the valley onto Spring Mountain. The fires destroyed dozens of winery buildings, homes and even some steep hillside vineyards.

While most of the vineyards weren't touched by the fires, smoke damage tainted the grapes still on the vines so badly that they became unusable. The fire climbed Sterling's steep hilltop, destroying many of the trees that had once shaded the buildings and leaving burn marks on the outside of the winery.

Fortunately, it did not go up in flames, although it destroyed the popular tramway, which was the only way to bring customers to the top. It took until October of 2023 for Sterling to reopen. After being part of a dynamic trio of destination wineries at the top of the valley, suddenly the Castello found itself the sole star in that constellation. That was true even though the hills surrounding it were covered with charred tree stumps, and their large storage building, filled with wine, was gutted by the fire. However, they got their doors open to visitors after that disaster remarkably fast. There is an advantage to being in a traditional stone building.

From the road El Castello sits hidden, on the far side of an impressive gate, up a long, steep, curving lane lined with trees and vines. As you approach, the building suddenly appears, a towering pile of stone at the top of the hill. An orchard of hundred-year-old Italian olive trees, and grazing sheep surround the building. The architecture includes some whimsical grace notes.

A favorite of mine are the small 'repair' bricks that were fit into 'damaged' addition that juts out over the eastern entrance to the cellar. There are also the bricked up 'old' doorways and crumbling towers that you expect to see in a Medieval Castle. It makes the statement that, *'Yes, we've taken hits and it's been hard, but we adapted to the times, and we are still here!'*

Chapter Five
The Prussians & Italians

They say that the story of Northern Napa starts with the story of the three Jakes, Prussian winemakers who arrived in Napa in the 1870's. To best tell their story we need to provide some context. When the first settlers arrived in any new land, they always claimed the properties near the waterways. That location came with advantages; first was water for irrigation, but equally important for the budding entrepreneurs, was easy access to the docks where ships brought needed supplies. That was also where farmers and craftsmen might find ship captains looking for goods they could ship. Those dockside areas eventually became places of commerce and fortunes were made by the owners of warehouses where the deals were struck between the farmers and the shippers.

The farther that each group settled from the docks, the longer and more expensive their route to the market. The Napa River runs the length of the county, but the location of the city, which was the northernmost place that a ship could reach, is at the bottom of the valley. Above that, an oxbow-shaped bend, with its undulating banks and shallows, makes passage impossible.

The oldest building in the valley, a beautifully restored adobe, belonged to a Sergeant in the Mexican army. It sits at the junction of the Silverado Trail and Soscol Avenue, once known as the 'Old Soscol Ferry Road.' All the land that the Sergeant could see was his, thanks to a land grant in gratitude for his service. He sold a *patch* of land to an American also named Jacob.

Jacob Coombs established downtown Napa, one of the first 'American' cities in California. He in turn sold land to other Americans and they wasted no time establishing the docks. Some of the oldest houses in that part of town were built by ship captains who transported produce from the valley to San Francisco and beyond. Once the docks opened optimistic settlers came from around the world, especially the French, Prussian and Italian winemakers. One of the most revered was the first of the winemaking Jakes, Jacob Beringer.

He and his brother Frederick had arrived in New York City to make beer for America's growing population. But Jacob, the younger brother and winemaker, heard about the wonderful wine grapes being grown in the North Bay region, so the brothers decided he should check the place out. If it looked like a sound investment,

Frederick, the money guy, would find investors in New York City.

Mark Twain has a wonderful commentary about who comes to California, *"America is built on a tilt, and everything loose eventually rolls to the Pacific."* The North Bay, more than most places, has benefitted from the efforts of big personalities, who coincidentally were often the youngest boys in the family. Why are the youngest children so often adventurers? Because traditionally, in European cultures, inheritance passed to the oldest son, so the younger siblings could either work for their elder brother or make their own way. Since the youngest son had the least to lose and were often accustomed to making their own way, that was who you often found on the frontiers where opportunity and risk co-existed.

So, Jake Beringer, the younger brother, headed to the frontier. When he arrived in Napa, he got a job working at the Charles Krug Winery. Krug was a Prussian socialist writer and philosopher, who had established his winery far from the river docks for a couple of reasons.

First, much of the best growing land to the south had already been grabbed by the Americans. Second, and more importantly, Krug had married the daughter of the notorious, quarrelsome and quite colorful Dr. Edward Bale. The young Miss Bale's dowry included several hundred acres of potentially prime farmland just north of downtown Saint Helena, which today is the site of Napa's oldest existing winery, Charles Krug, owned by the Mondavi family.

Bale was an English ship's physician who had been shipwrecked off the coast of Monterey at the sudden conclusion of his first voyage. He had fallen into a fortuitous position as the doctor to the Spanish Governor, because the previous physician had recently led a *revolt* against the Governor and now was persona non grata. As part of his duties, he served as the physician for the Presidio in San Francisco where he was known for producing remedies with a *remarkably* high amount of alcohol. This did not endear him to some of the local women, who were having a hard enough time managing the wild men who were drawn to this remote outpost, without the Doctor's nefarious potions.

However, that position led to him marrying General Vallejo's niece and being given a sizable land grant in Northern Napa, where he is known locally for funding the building of the *Bale Grist Mill*, outside Saint Helena. Bale also, for some weird reason, named his land grant 'Carne Humana,' or human flesh. He didn't stick around to explain, because when gold was discovered in the Sierra Madre Mountains, he *headed for the hills* and met his demise there.

Before starting his winery, Charles Krug worked for Count Haraszthy at Buena Vista in Sonoma, where he learned winemaking. The Count loaned Krug a small apple press to get him started. Krug neglected to return it and you can see it at Krug's Winery, built in the late 1800's. On the very entertaining historic tour at Buena Vista, the Count, recently portrayed by an actor in an ambassadorial role, seems to be especially pained by

Krug's oversight and the loss of his prodigal press. While Krug was the owner for only a brief time, his name is enshrined on Napa's oldest winery still in existence.

So, while Jacob Beringer worked for Krug, his brother Fredrick was making beer in New York City and pursuing that most 'New York-esque' of goals; raising money for the California winery his brother was envisioning. Eventually the brothers purchased land across the road from Krug and in 1876 built their winery on a slope above the road at the northern edge of downtown Saint Helena. They could reach the Napa River docks via the railroad tracks that ran the length of the valley. This made shipping their wine easy.

The Beringer Winery has the distinction of having *never missed a harvest*, even during Prohibition when they made wine for the churches, although they did hide bottles to avoid the 'unreasonable' taxes. They promptly forgot about that, because many years later, while doing repairs in the cave, they found caches of wine bottles hidden in walled up niches.

While Jacob Beringer was making a success within walking distance from the pretty town of Saint Helena, farther north outside Calistoga, the second Jake, Jacob Schram, was *'hoeing a harder row.'* Schram was a Prussian barber and winemaker who married a good German American girl, Annie Weaver. They were building the Schramsberg Winery, high on the slopes of the Mayacamas Mountain range, in an area known as Diamond Mountain. Even today, driving up the hill in a car, it's a steep climb from the valley floor. I can only imagine the number of curses that the trees along that drive heard, as wagons hauled loads of supplies up the mountain behind their straining teams of oxen and horses.

Being on the hills so far north brought an advantage. Hillsides made of volcanic ash are perfect for digging extensive caves for aging the wine. That backbreaking and dangerous kind of work was done by the Chinese miners who had been digging silver and mercury on the slopes of Mount Saint Helena and in the hills of Sonoma's Alexander Valley.

The Beringer wineries were built against the hillsides to accommodate a cave as well, but they don't compare to the deep caverns that have been bored into the hills behind the Schramsberg Winery. Clearly Jacob and Annie were bold thinkers, willing to take a risk and industrious enough to make it work.

In Northern Napa there was a wealthy San Francisco family called Coit. They owned a beautiful ranch that spanned from the Mayacamas to the west, across the valley floor and up into the Vaca hillsides to the east. This was just a short distance from the Schram winery. Their daughter, Lillie Coit, was a *San Fransico icon*. She was known as 'Fire Bell Lil,' because she was both the darling and the patroness of the San Francisco fire companies, who had saved her life several times. She was one of early San Francisco's great personalities.

Like many well-to-do city families, they had a home outside the foggy city to get away from the cold and damp and enjoy the warm summer sun in Napa. The Coit Ranch was quite the gathering place where renowned authors and prominent locals were often invited to socialize. In the days before television and the internet, if you can imagine such a time, card games were often featured in these gatherings.

Not surprisingly, their guests often included the local winemakers, who would always arrive with a bottle or two of their best wines. One night Jacob Schram and Jacob Beringer were engaged in a friendly game of poker in the Coit parlor. They were both holding good hands, and Jacob Schram bet two large, ornately carved winemaking tanks. But Lady Luck was smiling on Jacob Beringer that evening, and a couple of days later the two tanks, with the name Schramsberg, meaning Schram's Mountain, carved on the front, arrived on a wagon at the Beringer winery. They stayed there in the winery for almost *one hundred years*.

Now while the Beringer family managed to keep their very conveniently situated winery until the 1970's, the Schrams didn't endure the scourge of phylloxera as well, and the winery sat closed for many years. Finally, in 1965, the Davies family bought the property and began the slow process of bringing it back to life. In a surprise decision for the time, they decided to focus on producing sparkling wines by the traditional Méthode Champenoise under the name Schramsberg. About the same time, the Beringer family was in discussions to sell the winery to the Swiss food giant, Nestle.

As Chapter two of Jacob and Annie Schram's winery began with the new owners, there were only about twenty wineries in the valley. This was dramatically different from Jacob's time when there were over a hundred. In the 1960's, with so few wineries, if you were so inclined you could visit each one and expect a nice reception. Jaime Davies did just that, visiting her neighbors to learn what she could about the local wine business. Of course, she had to visit Jacob Beringer's Winery, where she was shown around by the head winemaker, Ed Sbragia, a big, friendly guy who grew up in Geyserville in Northern Sonoma.

They were walking through the caves and came upon these two, tall wooden tanks with the name Schramsberg carved on their faces. Jaime must have been a little shocked to see those two tanks, which were so obviously from 'her' winery, there in the Beringer cellar. She asked Ed about the tanks, and he told her about the card game between the two Jakes at Lillie Coit's house, and about who had the better hand.

By this time, almost a hundred years later the tanks were veritable antiques, and no longer usable for winemaking, but they were part of her winery's history. So, she asked Ed if she could buy them, but Ed said sorry, no! Jaime thought, 'That was that!' What she didn't know was that Beringer was about to close the deal with Nestle. Ed didn't want to have to say to the new owners, "Oh, those tanks weren't included in the price." More importantly, one of the qualities that made it an attractive deal for the Swiss was the Beringer history. When they took over, they worked hard to turn it into a major tourist destination with an extensive menu of historical tours.

Once the deal was completed, and Jacob Beringer's winery started its second chapter with the new owners, Jaime got a phone call from Ed Sbragia's secretary, who said, "Ed would like to invite you to a card game at the winery. You'll be *playing for those tanks* with the Schramsberg name on the front. Jaime's initial reaction was something like 'What on earth is this about?' But Jaime said she would be happy to come, and the secretary gave her a date and time, and suggested that she wear something nice.

A few weeks later Jaime showed up at the appointed time and place and there, on the broad walkway, in front of the winery was a card table, with all the accoutrements. Next to it, lit up like a stage set, were the two tanks, freshly cleaned and polished. Ed Sbragia and his assistant winemakers were here and there chatting with some photographers and Nestle executives.

Jaime had just *walked into a publicity event* designed to celebrate the colorful history of the winery. It seemed great to Jaime since she would get the tanks for free, but there was one hitch. She confided in Ed that she had never played poker in her life, so she was a little unsure about how she was going the win the jackpot. Ed reassured her saying, "Don't worry about it, you just *play the cards that we deal you.*" He had stacked the deck for her, so the tanks, after so many years away, would be going home.

The tour at Schramsberg has become one of our favorites because of its history, its unique aging caves with their stacked bottles stretching into the mountainside, and the natural beauty of the place. Today, when you take the tour of their caves the oversized pair of tanks sit side by side in a place of honor, looking quite happy to be back where they belong.

This was not the only time that luck figured into the wineries fate. Two events dramatically helped the winery cement its fortunes. In the late 1800's when Robert Louis Stevenson and his American bride Fanny honeymooned in Calistoga, the local stagecoach driver, Long John Silverado, brought them there for a visit. The young couple were thoroughly impressed by what the Schram's had accomplished, especially considering that Jacob, a Prussian immigrant, had been a barber with a shop in downtown Saint Helena.

He and Annie chose this hillside land because it was cheap enough that they could afford it. This was a different situation from Jacob Beringer with his financier brother. Schram's r*ag to riches story* on the far frontier so appealed to Stevenson that their winery was memorialized in his book, 'The Silverado Squatters,' which gained them some much appreciated attention.

Another stroke of luck happened a hundred years later, and it made a dramatic difference to the reborn winery's eventual success. In 1972, President Nixon and his Secretary of State, Henry Kissinger, organized an unannounced trip to open a diplomatic relationship with China. Nixon wanted to bring an American sparkling wine for the banquet. He was from California and wanted an American owned, California wine, of which there were very few, but luckily Nixon was familiar with

Schramsberg. So, Jaime gets a phone call from some guy at the State Department, explaining that they would like to buy twenty cases of their best 'Champagne.' What Jaime didn't tell him was that twenty cases would be *one fifth of the winery's production* that year. But happy for the sale, the winery folks loaded up a truck and drove over the eastern hills to Travis Airforce Base, where a crew put the wine on a plane and flew it to Washington DC. They eventually received the payment from the State Department, thank you very much!

But then, a few weeks later, the fireworks went off when Nixon and Kissinger landed in China! One of Jaime's friends called her on the phone and said, "Turn on the TV, Barbara Walters is in Tiananmen Square in Peking (as Beijing was known in the west at the time) holding up a bottle of your wine." Schramsberg gained instant fame in the wine world, for being part of this historic event, with the greatest endorsement possible. Not surprisingly, they sold out that entire year's production, and the next and the next, and their name became synonymous with great California sparkling wines.

While Jacob Beringer built his winery just outside the town of Saint Helena, and Jacob and Annie Schram built their estate just south of downtown Calistoga, the third Jake, named Jacob Grimm, yes, like the fairy tale author, built his winery north of Calistoga. He bought hillside land in a remote location, on the road to Sonoma's Knight's Valley. It had to be dirt cheap, but it was well chosen, because like the other two Jakes, he chose western hillsides for his winery, so the vines could take advantage of the morning sunshine. While Jacob Grimm had the longest ride the docks, *he also had the most beautiful views of Mount Saint Helena.* From the property today you can still see the old mine tailings on the slopes of that graceful mountain.

The winery is on a part of the road that has more winding sections than straight, and the entrance to Grimm's property is on rise. From there the land rises again on a gentle slope leading to a small hollow, where Jacob and his brother built the Grimm winery. From there the hillside rises steeply, so they cut trellises to plant the vines.

Unlike the vintners of Oakville, Rutherford and Saint Helena, with their nice level vineyards, the process of cutting trellises into hillsides, and farming those inclines can be back breaking work. This was in the days before ATV's, rototillers, tractors, backhoes and bulldozers. But the work paid off and the vineyards thrived, producing wonderful grapes for *almost a hundred years.*

Like the other two Prussian Jakes, Grimm brought in the Chinese hard rock miners to cut caves into the volcanic hills behind the crush pad, which are still used today. When you go inside it feels a little eerie because the walls are coated with a non-toxic mold that lines many of the ancient French caves. Even though they tell you it's not dangerous, there is something in human psychology that is cautious about mold and fungus.

Grimm farmed these beautiful, terraced hillsides for many years. While the winery eventually closed, the vineyards kept producing until the early 1960's, when a fire raging across the northern part of the county raced through the vineyards, reducing the vines and buildings to ash.

It was after that when a college history professor visited the denuded, terraced hill and decided that this would be a good place to raise his family and make wine. Realizing that he didn't know enough about the land, he hired the most prominent consultant in the area, the diminutive Russian André Tchelistcheff. André was the winemaker at both Beaulieu Vineyards and Buena Vista, and he laid out many of the region's most interesting vineyards.

André walked the hills and told the new owner that this land was *perfect for Zinfandel*. Now today, if any Napa consultant told a new vineyard owner that they should plant Zin they'd be fired. Half of the grapes in Napa today are of the 'big bucks' Cabernet Sauvignon variety, but it wasn't always like that. At one time Zinfandel and Petite Sirah were the dominant red grapes and the northern part of the valley especially enjoyed the steady heat that Zin adores. For growers, Zinfandel has the advantage of ripening early and producing a good red, medium bodied wine. In a competitive market, an early ripening grape can help a grower get to the market when there are more buyers who are looking to buy fruit and have pockets full of money.

All during the thirteen years of Prohibition, Italian immigrants on the East Coast and along the Great Lakes bought grapes for their homemade wines, and Zin was one of the four best shipping grapes. That's why north of the narrow neck of the Napa Valley, where the town of Saint Helena is located, there are still plenty of Zinfandel vines, distinctive due to their lack of trellises. But to get back to the Grimm Vineyards, based on what André recommended, the Professor and his family planted Zinfandel and five other varieties that would grow well there.

Besides marketability, there was a practical benefit that the selection produced. Because each variety ripened at a different time, and their location on the hillside further extended that timeline, they could harvest the entire sixty acres of vineyards over three months, with just four men.

On that steep hillside they depend on small ATV's and twenty-five-pound picking bins. They cart the grapes down the hill to where the Professor, now the winemaker, personally *tips the bins* into the tanks, making sure that every grape is as perfect as possible.

In an interesting confirmation of André's assessment, in recent years the scientists from the University of California at Davis, one of the world's most esteemed winemaking colleges, came by with an offer. They had solved a long-time problem that Zinfandel suffers from, uneven ripening in the bunches, using a new clone they developed.

In viticulture a clone is a natural mutation that develops from an existing vine. The leaves, fruit or root will exhibit different qualities from the mother plant. The growers will propagate it, to see if it has desirable properties. If it does, it may eventually replace the other vines in the field. All the vines you see in the vineyards today are clones, of clones, of clones, as growers sought better and better vines.

For generations Zinfandel growers had sought solutions to the problem of unripe, bitter grapes in bunches that were otherwise ready to be made into wine. When they threw in the entire bunches, those tart berries would affect the flavor. If they kept the grapes on the vine until the bunches were entirely ripe, the higher sugar levels produced *ballistic* alcohol that would dry out your palate with each sip. The third solution is a method used by high-end wineries, where the bunches are de-stemmed and the grapes are sorted individually, an expensive and labor-intensive way to eliminate those unripe berries.

The scientists at UC Davis had produced a Zinfandel clone where the bunches ripened evenly, and they wanted to plant a test vineyard, which would later belong to the winery. Why did they come to the Professor? Because they had determined that this was the best location in California for growing Zinfandel! Andre was right!

Jacob Grimm would have been pleased to see the dedication that his vineyards inspired, and the owner wanted to name it for him, calling it *the Grimm Winery*. That's not a surprising thought from a former history professor. But his children *overruled* him and after some discussion they chose something that connected the place to the third Prussian Jake, Storybook Mountain.

Chapter Six
Prohibition Changes the Game

When you live in an area where the industry revolves around wine, anything that affects the legality, acceptance, or even opinion about alcohol sends ripples through the community. Even today, when a state changes their shipping requirements to make it easier for wineries to ship their products, it's immediately in the industry news.

How much then did prohibition affect Wine Country? That's when the United States of America decided that after thousands of years of wine serving humanity so faithfully, alcohol consumption should be *illegal!* That affected the North Bay dramatically, on multiple levels and it left behind some interesting stories!

One of my *favorites* is about the Nichelini family, who have owned their winery in the far part of Napa's Chiles Valley for five generations. I've often thought of how poor, but determined those folks must have been to homestead in such a difficult place. The Chiles is a narrow valley surrounded by steep hillsides, and the old winery is perched on a ridge by the side of a narrow road. From the Silverado Trail, it's a 20-minute ride in a modern car up winding Sage Canyon Road just to reach them. How hard was it to establish a winery there when they depended on oxen and mule carts?

But even though it's a difficult location, it did have one big advantage. It is on the road that connects the heart of the Napa Valley, east through the hills to the Central Valley and the State Capitol of Sacramento. The other route from the upper valley takes you south through the city of Napa and around the mountains, which lengthens the trip considerably.

Back in the day, for people traveling through those narrow passes, the *only place to stop for lunch* was at Mrs. Nichelini's. She didn't cook anything custom, just served whatever she was making that day. But since this is Napa and everything grows well here, you could count on it being a satisfying meal. In the early years of prohibition, the local police occasionally ignored minor infractions, but the federal revenue agents were another matter. One day, two revenue agents were traveling from Sacramento to Napa, and they stopped in at Mrs. Nichelini's for lunch. The Missus put out a wonderful meal for them and being a good Italian-Swiss wife, Caterina put out two glasses of wine for the gentlemen. The two Revenue Agents enjoyed their meal, paid her, said thank you very much, and then *arrested* her for bootlegging.

Now this is farm country, where everybody knows everybody and people were incensed that they would arrest her, a friend and a mother. Of course, there was also the practical consideration of lunch. If she was in jail, there wasn't going to be any place to stop for food on the road back-and-forth to Sacramento. It caused such an uproar that the local Justice had to find a better solution.

So instead, they arrested her husband, Anton Nichelini, who was a bit of a hard case. That was seen as a better, although not ideal solution. The locals had suffered economic devastation due to this crazy law, so people felt that sending him to prison was completely unfair. So, the judge decided that he should serve his six-month term in the local jail, a short distance from his home.

The local sheriff wasn't happy about this either, so Anton wasn't *locked* in a cell. Instead, he helped around the place during the day. The fact that he shared the care packages from his wife's kitchen didn't hurt. There was one logistical problem, the sheriff didn't work weekends, so Anton would go home to his wife and a pile of chores. For an industrious farmer and miner like him, his six-month term was the closest thing he ever got to a vacation. Hopefully, they timed it for the winter when the vines were asleep, because his neighbors depended on him for grapes and bottles of good wine.

My *second favorite* story from prohibition is about how Samuele Sebastiani, whose winery was a short walk from the Sonoma Plaza, ingeniously dealt with this potential disaster. Sam had built his winery in 1906, so by the time prohibition happened in late 1919 he was well-established. The first thing he did in reaction to this horrible news was to fill out the application to make wine for the Catholic churches and the Jewish Temples. Like most Italian immigrants, he was a devoted Catholic and those services include wine, in memory of Jesus's first miracle, turning water into wine.

Yes, according to the Bible, *Jesus was a winemaker!* There are also numerous parables about tending vineyards including the story of Adam and Eve. When their sons, Cain and Abel went looking for work, one became a shepherd while the other tended vines. What kind of vines do you think those were? If the government attempted to restrict the use of wine by the churches and temples, they would have been interfering with their freedom of religion, the bedrock upon which America was founded. So that's not happening!

Over in Napa, George LaTour, the owner of Beaulieu Vineyards, also got the permit to make wine for the churches. But *he had a special connection!* Just up the road was a large estate owned by the arch diocese of San Francisco, and George was friends with the archbishop. The church would send troubled kids from the city to work on the farm. Today that property is owned by the Round Pond Winery, and as you travel across Rutherford Road you can see the old chapel left behind from those days. George asked the archbishop for a letter of introduction to parishes in need of sacramental wine throughout the country.

While all of La Tour's neighbor wineries closed, except for Beringer and Christian Brothers, a religious brotherhood, Beaulieu Vineyards expanded. While Prohibition was hard on Wine Country, it was *fantastic* financially for the churches and temples, where membership boomed. There were reports of Jewish temples in New York City that grew five times over, and they suddenly included many new families named O'Donnell, O'Leary and Murphy.

But to get back to Sam Sebastiani, at a time when many people were ripping out vines and planting the Italian plum trees used for prunes, Sam and his friends were buying up vineyards. That's because Prohibition happened during the second great wave of Italian migration to the United States. The first wave started in the late 1800's, the second started after the First World War and the third took place in the 1960's.

Most people don't realize that the Italians were one of the *single largest migrations* ever to come to the United States. Sixty million Italians came in three great waves and pizza has been one of America's favorite foods ever since. Amazingly, more Italians left their country for the Americas than live in Italy today. Many of them settled along the East Coast and the shores of the Great Lakes and while some of them were winemakers, all were wine drinkers. When I was growing up in New Jersey, where forty percent of the population was descended from Italy, I used to hear, *"All those old Italians make wine"!* It turns out they were right. That's because, starting in the 1800s, phylloxera attacked the Italian vines and the wine industry, which employed 80% of working people, mostly collapsed. Anyone who could leave the country did, looking for work!

When Congress passed the law banning alcohol, they made a cut out for the home winemaker, I think in part because of the large numbers of Italians, who were a pretty tough lot and many of them carried knives! At first the wine could only have about 1% alcohol, but that lasted about five minutes, and they quickly raised it to a more reasonable 8% to 9%, but with the home winemakers, who was checking? Every neighborhood had their local winemaker. *I know this because* my grandfather was his community's winemaker and he made wine for them for over 40 years. During prohibition, a local winemaker would gather the names of the families they were making wine for, and each could get up to *two hundred* gallons per year, which is a lot of wine. My father, who was my grandfather's youngest child, told me about going down to the rail lines in the Iron Bound section of Newark with his father, to buy boxes upon boxes of grapes.

Before going to school in the morning, he and his brothers did the punch downs where they would push the floating grapes down into the juice, to infuse it with flavor and color. In the off season, they would take the barrels apart, clean and reassemble them. Even back then, good winemaking was mostly about cleanliness, and having five sons was a big advantage.

Meanwhile, back in California, Samuele Sebastiani, along with the Mondavis and the Gallos, recognized that these winemakers, their fellow Italians, would need grapes. So, while the Americans were tearing out vines, the Italian Americans were planting more, and during prohibition, wine grape production in Sonoma tripled.

So now, besides making church wine, Sam was shipping grapes to the East Coast. You would think that this just allowed them to survive, but in fact Prohibition was a boon to the Italian American growers, because the home winemakers at the other end of that rail line, would pay more for grapes than their local wineries had ever paid. By the time Prohibition ended the Italian American growers owned extensive vineyards in prime locations throughout the state and those Italian American families have *dominated* the California wine industry since then.

But making wine for the churches and shipping grapes wasn't the only part of Sam's Prohibition strategy. When he made wine for the churches, the alcohol was taxed immediately. On the day when the grapes were put in the tank, the taxman would come by. They would calculate the volume of juice, and the amount of sugar, and from those amounts they would determine how much alcohol was going to be made. They would calculate the tax and Sam would write the check and the taxman would leave.

What the tax man didn't know was that Sam had dug tanks underneath the floor of the winery. Then his pipefitter installed hidden valves and pipes on the backs of the tanks.

After the taxman left, they would open the secret valves and send that wine into the tanks under the floor. Then they would bring in *more grapes* to fill the upper tanks. This way Sam only paid half the tax, and by the time Prohibition was over, they had 600,000 gallons of wine aging under their floors. I'll bet the day after Prohibition was repealed Sam was sending that wine out in tanker cars to a thirsty country.

For an interesting insight into the United States alcohol laws, this taxation system still exists in the perfume industry. A cosmetics company will have a tank of alcohol on site, and each day they will pull a certain amount out and mix it with flower oils and other ingredients to create their perfumes. At the end of the day, they calculate the tax on the alcohol they've used and put a check in the mail to the alcohol tax bureau.

The wine and spirits industry still works under the shadow of *restrictive* laws carried over from the Prohibition era. That's why most American wineries don't have distilleries onsite, as is common in Europe, where they can hydrate their left-over pomace to make low cost, high-alcohol beverages like French marc, Italian grappa, Spanish orujo and Portuguese bagaço.

Unfortunately, not every California winery had such an inventive and painless solution to Prohibition. In Northern Sonoma, on the edge of the town of Healdsburg, the Simi Winery, started by two Italian friends, had done very well for many years, buying land and building a large winery. Both partners passed away and one of their daughters was left to guard their legacy.

When Prohibition began, the feeling among many of the Italian winemakers, for whom wine was in their blood, was that this was an impossible law and that it couldn't last. Italian culture by its very nature is *patient*, so many people felt they could wait it out until these foolish people in Washington DC came to their senses.

The daughter wasn't willing to risk Sam's strategy, and selling grapes alone was not bringing in enough revenue to sustain them, so over the course of the thirteen years she sold pieces of land to pay the taxes and cover the expenses required to keep the winery whole. By the time Prohibition was over, their operation was much smaller, but they had endured, and they were still on their feet! The winery has changed hands over the years, but you can visit it and taste their wines when you travel to Healdsburg in Northern Sonoma.

An often-told story in southern Napa is about the black chickens of the Biale Family Winery. This is not a Prohibition story, but instead about how the locals felt about the government taxing something as divinely essential as wine. In the early days of telephone service, those spread-out farmhouses were connected by 'party lines.'

When you were on the phone, your neighbors could pick up their phone and hear your conversation. It provided a great deal of entertainment, like today's social media, for bored farm wives and children who spent too much time cut off from their neighbors. You knew that if you had any secrets, you shouldn't talk about them on the phone because they wouldn't be secrets for long.

For the Italians wine is food, so they didn't understand why it should be taxed any differently from carrots? Luckily, Napa and Sonoma, before and after Prohibition, were filled with what today we call artisan winemakers. These are small family affairs that have passed down the skills for generations. So, if you wanted to buy some wine without having to pay those pesky taxes, you could find someone to sell it to you. But one of the problems with a small wine producer is that *they run out of wine*. So, the best thing to do before you hopped in your truck and headed over the rough country roads was to call them up on the phone and see if they had any wine left. How do you ask them about that when your neighbors could be listening in on your conversation?

The answer to that requires a little history. The Biale family, whose farm and winery are on Big Ranch Road in Napa's Oak Knoll District, in the southeastern part of the valley, grew kitchen vegetables that they sold at the local market. As is common with a small farm, they also raised chickens. This home business supplemented what the father earned as a miner in the distant mountains. But then he died in a mining accident, leaving the family in desperate straits. The oldest son, who was only twelve years old, announced to his mother that he would make wine for sale, and he did. When they drove their wagon full of vegetables to the markets, they hid the bottles of tax-free wine under the produce.

As his wine got better, Biale became known as one of the places to buy good wine tax free. But that was illegal, so they developed a code. When their neighbors called on the party line looking for wine, they knew to ask, "Do you have any *'black chickens'* for sale?" If they said 'yes,' they could head on over and buy a couple of bottles. Biale eventually became a legal, bonded winery, as did their neighbors, the Regusci family, located just a couple of miles north of the Biale's winery on the Silverado Trail.

At one time the 'Trail' passed right in front of the Regusci's big stone barn, built by Captain John Grigsby in the late 1800s. Today the Trail travels further to the west on a more level part of the valley floor. During Prohibition, Grandpa Regusci had his own home-based solution to the 'crazy law.' He built a still in a side room in the barn and brewed bottles of *'hooch'* for sale. Whenever he had some ready, he would leave a lamp on in the little peak window at the top of the barn where people driving by could see it shining from a distance.

The reality was, Prohibition was *disastrous* for the overall health of the nation. Before it was enacted most of the country was drinking healthy, low alcohol beverages like wine, beer and hard cider. In the cities those were often preferred to the water coming out of the taps, which was not always as safe to drink. Before Prohibition, most apples went into cider and they were only popularized to eat as raw fruit, in pies and as apple sauce when the hard cider businesses were shut down.

The reasons for Prohibition had less to do with alcohol and more to do with society's propensity for war. At the end of the Civil War, during which a bizarre number of American soldiers were killed and wounded, the main tool that veterans had for dealing with post-traumatic stress was alcohol. Hard liquor was more common in the cities and after returning from the war, husbands, fathers and sons by the thousands disappeared into bars.

It was a blight that left families destitute. That was when the 'Temperance' movement started, but then there was the Spanish American War, during which most of the fatalities were due to tropical diseases. Then sixteen years later came the incredibly brutal trench warfare of World War One. When the Temperance crusaders saw veterans coming home after that trauma, and heading for the bars, those childhood memories of the years after the Civil War were surprisingly fresh. Women especially knew what was going to come next and it gave them the impetus to push the eighteenth amendment through in 1919. To give you a time marker, women got the right to vote with the nineteenth amendment in 1920.

The problem was, wine and beer has been part of human nutrition for *millennia* for good reasons, people like to drink it, it makes them feel better, removes their aches and provides some significant health benefits. Hard alcohol was a more recent arrival in Europe, and this was not the first disaster it had created. But because wine required more time to make and was bulky to transport, the very profitable, illicit bootlegging business shifted towards making and smuggling hard liquor. For people who understood the basics of fermentation it was simple to make. All you needed was a pile of corn or grain, some water and yeast, and a small still you could build yourself.

You could make a variety of high proof liquors in a *fraction* of the time required to make wine and pour it into smaller bottles that were easier to hide and transport than those big wine jugs. During Prohibition, the east side of the city of Napa, where the Italians lived, was a hidden forest of stills. Every now and then people would hear explosions from that neighborhood, followed by the bell of the fire trucks.

They knew that the swirly copper tube on the top of someone's still had clogged up and the tank had dramatically burst its seams. It was estimated that New York City had as many as a *hundred thousand* speakeasies and tens of thousands of illegal stills supplying them. Even after prohibition in the United States, there continues to be plenty of clandestine stills producing tax free liquor.

As you drive up the Napa Valley these days, just as you pass the 'Welcome to Napa Valley' sign on the left, you can see the Far Niente winery sitting beyond it, surrounded by its vineyards. During Prohibition it was owned by a wealthy woman who had been widowed, and married a younger, handsome, and quite dashing WWI flying ace. Someplace in that big winery there was a still, because the Ace built an airstrip, so he could make deliveries with his plane.

As time went on and he got busier and busier, he added two more strips so he could always take off into the wind. Unfortunately, his stepdaughter hated this enterprising pilot and poisoned him. Eventually, family dysfunction and Prohibition got the better of them and the building was boarded up and silent for almost sixty years, Finally, the Nickel family revived the property and dug the first *new caves* in Napa in the 20th century.

As the country abandoned wine, beer and cider in favor of hard liquor, liver disease and alcoholism skyrocketed. This campaign by the 'sobriety crusaders' had produced horrible, unintended consequences, damaging the society they were trying to help. It also produced fortunes for bootleggers and the rise of the criminal class.

One legal remnant of those thirteen years is a pile of regulations related to alcohol production that requires wineries to have compliance officers to keep the paperwork current. Another remnant is a bizarrely convoluted alcohol distribution system, which was set up after Prohibition by Meyer Lansky, the Mob's accountant. For many years, if a company wanted to have their wine or liquor distributed in a city, they would have to bring an envelope of cash to grease the wheels with the distributor.

The third remnant of Prohibition was effectively a ban on home beermaking that persisted until the Carter administration. While home winemaking continued through Prohibition, thanks to its connections with the Bible, beermaking was completely shut down. However, the regulations related to beer were so draconic that even after Prohibition was repealed, only the largest companies could handle all the requirements to have a brewery. Why was Congress *so hard* on the beermakers?

Because Prohibition became law in 1919, right after the First World War when the lawmakers were still mad at the German American families who owned many of the breweries. But then, during the Carter administration, the regulations were relaxed and home beermaking became legal again.

That was when we saw the growth of the Micro-Brewery, especially in Sonoma. Why? Because winemakers are traditionally beer drinkers! After an entire day of working with wine, that's the last thing they want to drink. Instead, they prefer to relax with a nice, cold glass of beer. Sonoma also had a long tradition of growing superior hops, and these Sonoma winemakers had all the equipment necessary to make their own beer, and so they did. After a while they got good at it, and the artisan brewery was born.

During Prohibition, while the large Italian population in Sonoma expanded their vineyards, the growers in Napa went in a different direction. In Napa, where there was a larger percentage of Americans, Prussians and French vintners, they were concerned with being seen as disreputable, because they were producing grapes that could be made into wine.

Their main profits came from winemaking, so south of Saint Helena, farmers ripped out vineyards and planted fruit and nut trees or brought in cattle or sheep to graze. Today there are still sections of both counties devoted to cattle, sheep, goats and horses. In the northern part of the valley there was a large population of Italian American growers. Many had arrived looking for work as masons and laborers. Growing grapes was in their blood, so they kept their Zinfandel vineyards, shipping their grapes to the East Coast in box cars filled with dry ice.

However, there were so many people who understood fermentation, that the speakeasies of Napa became a favorite destination for folks from the city seeking a fun time. Those unlit, winding country roads, filled with drunk drivers, were littered with crashes. The shame of Prohibition is that Napa and Sonoma's hundreds of wineries had been producing an abundance of healthy wines, and thanks to this short-sighted, misguided policy, it would be forty years before a new crop of wineries would blossom in those beautiful valleys.

Chapter Seven
Judging California in Far Off Paris

As tour guides tell it, the Judgment of Paris is a simple story. In June of 1976, a competition was held in Paris pitting the top California wines against the top French wines. The Californians, most notably, the 'Napans,' routed the *'Frenchies'* and put our little Valley on the world-wide wine map. Pretty simple, yes?

But of course, in Wine Country, there's always more to the story and the genuinely interesting pieces are stuck in various memories all over both counties. The story has been told countless times by tour guides and winery hosts. It was even made into a small budget, but popular movie that was shot on location called 'Bottle Shock.' It was seen by a surprisingly large number of people thanks to the airlines featuring it on California bound flights. I've heard all kinds of inside stories about both the 'Judgment' and the movie, thanks to being both a local guide and television producer. At the wine and travel writer's conference at Saint Helena's Meadowood Resort, I spent quite a bit of time with the original screenwriter, Ross Schwartz, hearing about how the story turned into a movie.

Ross is an entertainment attorney in Los Angeles, and his father was a prominent television producer whose credits included Gilligan's Island. It seems to me that if you live in Los Angeles and you have connections to the industry, you must write a movie script. Well, Ross wanted to try his hand at writing one, so his wife told him about this wacky story she heard about the American wines beating the French wines back in 1976. When Ross looked into it, he realized that the owner of Chateau Montelena, Jim Barrett, was, like Ross, an attorney.

Jim had given up his San Francisco law practice to pursue his dream of producing a great wine at the top of the Napa Valley. Even better for the sake of the story, previous to their win, the winery was on the ropes. Even in that precarious situation, Jim *didn't want his wines included* in the tasting, because in the previous years the French had always taken the highest scores. He didn't want to give this English shop owner and his French wine writers the opportunity to pump up their wines at the expense of the Americans.

But unbeknownst to him, his son Bo snuck some bottles out of the winery and got them on the plane. When they won top honors, the new fame brought them a surge of business as New York restaurants called wanting to put 'Montelena' on their lists. This was the kind of great underdog story that Americans love. So, Ross writes the script, and one day while delivering a contract to a friendly producer he mentions it, asking if they would like to take a look. The producer said yes, so Ross sent it over.

A little while later they called Ross and said, "It's a great script, but it's *only going to cost three or four million* to produce, and we don't do anything less than fifty. But my production manager is going to call you and explain why we can't do it." Now Ross thought that was a little strange, so he said, "I understand, he doesn't need to call me." But his producer friend said, "It's no problem, you see, my production manager really likes the story, so he's going to call you."

A couple of days later he gets a call from the production manager, who says, "It's too small for us, *but I have friends* who produce the Sonoma Film festival. They know everyone up there that you need to know to get this made, so I sent them the script. If they say yes, they want to do it, we'll arrange the financing." Now Ross thought, this is getting interesting.

A while after meeting Ross, I interviewed the movie's co-producer for our TV show 'Wine Country at Work'. Marc and Brenda Lhormer had been in the Silicon Valley events business until they moved to Sonoma and became co-directors of the already existing Sonoma Film Festival. Marc gave me the next part of the story.

"I got a call from a fella I met through the Film Festival.

He told me about the script and suggested that we produce it. I told him that we weren't movie producers, and we didn't know how to do that! He told me that with a movie like this it's about two things. First you find the right people, and second you connect with the people in charge of the locations where you want to film. Well, through the festival we've met plenty of directors, actors and videographers, and we knew all the people in charge of the places in Sonoma where we would need to film. Then he said, 'If you'll produce the movie, we'll find the financing!' How could we say no?"

As they began the project, an unexpected player entered the game. George Taber, the writer who reported the story and authored a book about the 'Judgement', was in talks with a producer. The movie would focus, in big part, on Montelena's Croatian American winemaker, Mike Grgich. Ross's script focused on the relationship between Jim and Bo Barrett, and while Mike was a character, *he was not the star*. So, Mike said he didn't want to be mentioned in their film.

After the 'Judgement' in 1976 Mike cofounded the Grgich Hills Winery on July 4th, 1977. Not surprisingly, with that other production in their rear-view mirror, Marc and Brenda became focused on their film being first to market. While the story was centered on Napa and Paris, the movie was filmed in Sonoma, except for one fun scene at Montelena. It is the only segment where there is a visual reference to Mike Grgich. In it a pretty blonde intern is hosing down a big wood basket press on the crush pad while a group of men sit on the wall watching. One of the smaller actors sported a vest and a *beret* like Mike wore every day. Since the movie needed a winemaker, they included Mike's Mexican American assistant, Gustavo Brambila. After the movie came out Gustavo opened his own tasting room in downtown Napa while Marc and Brenda went on to found the Napa Film Festival.

The story that most guides tell is only quasi true. That's not to say that the American wines didn't resoundingly prove themselves against the French, because they did! The French complained that the wines were too young, and with proper aging they would prevail. So to prove that the tasting wasn't a fluke, various groups have repeated it more than thirty times over the years with the original wines. The Californians have *prevailed* every time, although it hasn't always been the same California wines that came out on top.

The reason for their success is simple. Wines are made in the vineyard. Napa and Sonoma are further south so they get warmer daytime weather than the vineyards of France. Also, their grapes get rain free skies for most of the growing season, which the French vintners could only dream about. Great wine grapes require very bright sunlight to produce rich flavors and deep colors. Napa and Sonoma sit immediately north of the shallow, *reflective* San Pablo Bay, which throws even more sunshine into the valleys.

The unique combination of having coasts along both the bay and the ocean produces the chilly nights that allow the grapes to hold on to their flavors and vital structure. Just off the coast are some of the deepest canyons in the Pacific Ocean, and when that frigid water wells up and encounters the hot sunshine it produces the famous Bay Area fog banks.

These flow up the valley nightly during the driest time of the year and coat the grapevines with cool water, which evaporates quickly in the morning sun. From the point of view of a grapevine, Napa and Sonoma simply have better growing conditions.

The name, 'The Judgment of Paris' implying a competition, first appeared as the title of an article in the revered New York Times. It was a *misnomer*, because the event was an annual wine tasting to celebrate the longtime friendly relationship between the two countries, where the French wines consistently outshone the Americans. It was sponsored by a British wine shop owner, Steven Spurrier who was also a partner in the Academy of Wine in Paris, which was France's first significant school focused on tasting and evaluating wine.

George Taber covered the tasting for the *New York Times* because he liked hanging out at the shop for the free samples. If the idea of a Brit owning a wine shop in Paris seems odd to you, it shouldn't. While the French have centuries of experience making wine, dating back to when the invading Celts and Romans arrived with vines in their wagons, the French didn't typically transport it beyond their shores.

It was the British who were their best customers, and it was the British ships that carried the French bottles to customers throughout Europe and the world. The wine from Madeira, where the British frequently bought wine to sell in India, was magically improved by the long, hot sea journey, rolling around in the belly of British sailing ships. My English clients are always more knowledgeable about the world's wines than either my French or Italian clients. While those two countries are the biggest wine producers, the makers tend to know their own region's well, but don't often look beyond their own backyard.

During the movie shoot we were living in Sonoma, and we watched the production crew turn the downtown around the Plaza into Paris. Meanwhile, our son Julian, who was connected to the theater union, was involved in building the sets.

During my years of touring, I've visited all the vineyards where the grapes were grown in both Sonoma and Napa, and the vineyards and wineries where the movie was shot and met numerous people who were involved in the original 'Judgment' and the movie, so I thought I had a pretty good handle on the story.

But then I read a wonderful article by Esther Mobley, of the *San Francisco Chronicle*, where she gave credit to the women who were the unsung heroes of this saga. At the time of the tasting in Paris a young American woman, Patricia Gastaud-Gallagher, was a partner in the Académie du Vin.

Patricia was in charge of organizing the annual French American tastings each year. Remember, it was the French that helped a young America throw off the British yoke, so you couldn't expect a Brit to handle that particular wine celebration.

Patricia had previously been hamstrung by the quality of the New York State wines that she could get from her friends at the American Embassy. They had heard that America's best wines were being grown in California, but production was still small, and they were not exporting bottles to Europe.

It was 1976, the year of America's Bi-Centennial and Patricia was a member of the 'Daughters of the American Revolution', a club that traces their families back to colonial times. Not surprisingly, she wanted to make that year's tasting *special*. Where to start? She contacted a California wine writer for suggestions, who put her in touch with a woman tour guide, Joanne Dickenson DePuy, who lived in Northern California. Joanne brought groups of California winemakers to France, so she knew all the important winemakers in Napa and Sonoma.

Luckily for the Californians, the Brits are always up for traveling for the sake of wine, so, a month before the event, Spurrier and his wife Bella visited Napa. Joanne drove them around the valley to her favorite wineries where they tasted the recent vintages and selected bottles for the event.

Steven and Bella paid *full price* for the bottles, even though they were offered an industry discount. Of course, the bottles only cost about five or six dollars at the time. Quite a difference compared to what they are going for now. Stephen and Bella headed back to Europe confident their bottles would be shipped.

As the time for the tasting session neared it looked like the bottles would be tied up in customs for who knew how long? Luckily, Joanne, *tour guide extraordinaire,* came to their rescue. She was about to embark on a tour with a group of local winemakers to France. At that time, airline passengers were permitted to carry two bottles of wine in their carryon luggage, so Joanne arranged for her guests to carry Spurrier's bottles. That was a critical decision because the wines were carried by people who knew a thing or two about handling bottles, and they arrived in close to pristine condition. Transportation is not wine's best friend.

As an aside, for many years Americans who drank French wines in America, and especially on the west coast, rarely had a true impression of those vintages unless they tasted them in France. That's because the wines were shipped in unrefrigerated containers where the heat often destroyed the flavors, especially when the ships traversed the tropics on the way through the Panama Canal. It was only when the high-end distributors started springing for the cost for refrigerated containers that the west coast market for French wines exploded.

In the Bay Area, premium wineries won't ship bottles during the hottest weather. I often tell my clients that when they taste wines at the winery, they are at their best. When a bottle of wine is transported over a long distance it can suffer from *bottle shock,* from which the movie took its name.

The combination of shaking and temperature changes locks up the aromas and flavors. It's best to wait for a week or so for the wine to recover so that wonderful personality can return! And it does!

So, the wine bottles were hand delivered to Stephen well before tasting. He had tasted the California wines where they were made, and the experience must have convinced him that they could compare well with the French wines. So, *at the last minute,* he did something quite different from previous tastings. He covered the bottles with paper bags, so the tasting wouldn't be colored by the judge's history with the labels.

The tasting begins and the judges, a collection of important French wine writers, taste their way through the many selections, recording their scores as they go. During the tasting they're commenting back and forth, claiming to recognize certain wonderful French vintages and brands. Finally, all the scores were handed in and the paper bags were taken off the bottles. As the scores were tabulated, everyone realized that the French judges had given *the highest scores* to two American wines, the Chateau Montelena Chardonnay, and the Stag's Leap Wine Cellars Cabernet Sauvignon.

It upset one of the critics so much that she grabbed her scores back, and her friend Patricia completely understood why. What she intended as an educational, comparative tasting, to celebrate American French Unity, Spurrier and Taber were spinning as a competition. A few days later Taber's article appeared on the *front page* of the New York Times, the respected and influential town crier for a city that, at that time, consumed much more imported wine than Californian!

Part Two

While the French paid this event little attention, it was a big deal to the Americans. Understanding its significance in the global wine market requires looking at the context. France, like most of Western Europe, has a long tradition of growing grapes and making wine. For centuries wine had been the only safe, potable and storable beverage other than pure well and spring water from the countryside.

In the cities wine was added to water so the alcohol could make it safe. But then ships brought *coffee* from Arabia, *tea* from China and *chocolate* from south America, all drinks that were high in antioxidants and caffeine. More importantly, they were made with boiled water that killed most pathogens. Then the Dutch brought Arabian *distilling technology* from Spain, where it was used to make perfumes and medicines. But in Northern Europe and England, they used it to produce cheap *Gin* from grains and juniper berries.

In England, the combination of that intoxicating drink, so much stronger than beer, ran into the industrial revolution, which dispossessed generations of country craftspeople. This suddenly impoverished class moved to the cities looking for work, where many turned to thievery and Gin to survive. As increasing crime overwhelmed the jails, retired naval ships of the line were moored in London Harbor as prisons. These horrifically housed prisoners became the first unwilling immigrants to the Australia penal colony on the other side of the world, that fortunately, turned out to be a wonderful place to grow wine grapes.

Faced with this new competition from these various drinks for the first time, the winemakers had to *'up their game'* to survive. While the more remote winemakers, like those in Burgundy struggled, the French vintners in Bordeaux, with their ready access to seaports and their British shipping partners, continued to thrive in this new, global market. Many of their most revered wineries date their first great vintages from this period, when they started playing for keeps. So, by 1976, the French winemakers were bringing centuries of experience to Spurrier's wine shop in Paris, making them a sure bet against the newbie Americans.

It seemed *implausible* that the California winemakers could take the top honors, Montelena and Stag's Leap were only recently started and were depending on grapes that other people had planted. What's equally amazing is that Bay Area wineries took multiple spots in the top five for both the red and white wines. The rich wine culture they have today was a California dream for the future, but suddenly that dream seemed much more possible. Remember, at the time this was happening, the California Wine Country looked like the Wild West, with growers wearing *cowboy hats* and driving pickup trucks.

The Californian's did have a couple of ringers. First among them was Russian born, French trained André Tchelistcheff, today called the Godfather of California winemaking. Andre laid out many of the important vineyards in the region and consulted widely with vintners, while directing winemaking at both Beaulieu Vineyards and Buena Vista in Sonoma. His trusted assistant for many years was Mike Grgich. They connected in part because Andre, besides speaking Russian, French and English, also spoke Croatian.

Here is another funny coincidence. Joanne Dickenson DePuy had been trying to unsuccessfully to convince André to lead a tour to France with her. He resisted until his wife convinced him to do it. Dorothy Tchelistcheff was a native Californian, a few years his junior, who ran their business behind the scenes. She knew that the connections they would make during a tour would be good for their consulting business. The three of them were busy herding a group of winemakers around France at the time of the tasting, when news of the results reached them while they were having lunch at a winery in Bordeaux.

Despite the fact that this was shockingly good news, especially since some of the winemakers in the Judgment were in the group, Andre insisted that they not make any fuss to avoid insulting their hosts. But the moment they got back on the bus celebrations *erupted*.

Wine was not the big business in Napa and Sonoma that it is today. There were more *plum* trees than grapevines in Napa and more *apple* trees in Sonoma. But great wines had been produced there before, starting in the late 1800's. As they considered their future, the question in the mind of many North Bay growers was whether or not there was a market for their high-quality wines? During WWII, when the European wineries were out of

America's reach, the more established wineries found a small market for the premium bottles they produced. But once the war ended, the European winemakers broke through the cellar walls where they had hidden their best wines. Pretty soon their labels reappeared on the restaurant wine lists.

That argument about whether the North Bay growers should make premium, or jug wines was the source of the famous feud between the Mondavi brothers. Robert wanted to aim for the stars while Peter wanted to keep their feet firmly on the Earth. That's not surprising considering that Robert was the marketer while Peter was the grower and winemaker.

When Robert left Charles Krug, which was the family business, he started the Robert Mondavi Winery in 1966. *His first winemaker was Warren Winarski, who four years later founded Stag's Leap Wine Cellars.* There Warren crafted the 1973 Cabernet Sauvignon blend that earned the highest red wine score at the 'Judgment.'

You can understand why the California grape growers are risk averse. In the late 1800's and the 1970's the root louse, Phylloxera, decimated their vines. Then in 1919, Prohibition closed all but a handful of wineries. In the following thirteen years bootleggers converted society to hard liquor, stealing their market. Many of them abandoned vineyards, and instead planted fruit and nut trees, or brought in livestock. The rest survived by selling grapes to the home winemakers, and the occasional jug of homemade to their neighbors.

At the time of the 'Judgment', some growers were making small amounts of premium wine, in part to show that they could. Warren's winery was in the Stags Leap district, located in the southeastern corner of the Valley. Until the 'Judgment' it was considered a backwater among the growers. That's because most of the work at that time was done from the seat of a tractor, so the growers preferred vineyards like those in Oakville and Rutherford, where they could drive straight and level for a long way before they had to turn around.

Stags Leap is filled with slopes and cut by canyons. *The small amount of level land near the river quickly rises into the rocky bench lands at the foot of the eastern hills.* It was not considered prime territory, until suddenly one of the local wines was on the front page of the New York Times. Then everybody paid attention!

The same conditions that made the vineyards less attractive for tractor farmed jug wines, makes it perfect for premium grapes, because all those nooks and crannies bounce the sunlight around and capture the evening fog, so it lingers through the morning. As the sunlight streams through the mist, the refracting colors enrich the flavors, adding fruity complexity.

As the hot sun sets on the western facing vineyards, the heat makes the vines pull more sulfur from the soil to deal with the heat. This turns into tannins that help the wine age properly. So, you get the bright fruit at the top and the woody flavors that create a solid foundation underneath. The complexity is surprising and enthralling!

But there's more to the story because an American Chardonnay also scored the highest, in a field filled with spectacular bottles. Chateau Montelena was an unlikely champion for Chardonnay because Calistoga is the *hottest* part of the valley. For generations, the local farmers focused on heat-loving Zinfandel and there are still plenty of those distinctive vineyards to be found there, with their cute, shrub shaped vines. But Chardonnay thrives in a cooler climate, and if you have the money, you can buy grapes. So, Jim Barrett, who, together with partners had revived Montelena 1972, told their winemaker, Mike Grgich, to find some Chardonnay grapes, because Chard was always a good seller.

Mike found the grapes over the mountains on the cool Sonoma benchlands above the Russian River. Even though this is not a great distance from Calistoga as the crow flies, the climate is dramatically different. It gets more of the cool breezes and fogs that roll in from the Pacific Ocean, and it's bisected by the cold Russian River that descends from the northern mountains of Mendocino.

The vineyards are moderately warm and dry during the day, but prone to cool fogs overnight that drench the vines with dew. The mix of extremes makes this a tremendous growing area for all kinds of plants. The famous botanist, Luther Burbank, did much of his work in nearby Santa Rosa, including creating a potato variety to save Ireland from the blight. He said that, of any place he had ever visited, Sonoma County was "the chosen spot of all the earth as far as nature is concerned." And he called the Redwood Empire, the great forests that blanket the Pacific coast, *the place "most blessed by nature."*

Today, the region is home to numerous Pinot Noir and Chardonnay vineyards, but at the time of the Judgment of Paris, it was mostly apple orchards and hops that covered the hills. The vineyards were mostly in the warmer Dry Creek Valley, farmed by Italian American families who grew Zinfandel and Olive trees, because it's truly impossible to live any kind of good life without wine and olive oil, or so I've been told.

The Chardonnay grapes came from the Bacigalupi family vineyards, which sit where the southern edge of the warm Dry Creek Valley meets the northern edge of the cool Russian River Valley. This transitional zone is capable of great complexity and the family has owned their little piece of paradise since 1956. There is a wonderful photo of Mike and Helen Bacigalupi, neither of which are very tall, standing in front of the vines that towered over them.

Mike was famous for being a *hard* bargainer, but Helen was nobody's fool, so I imagine they came to a fair price for those five tons of grapes that Helen had to deliver to 'Montelena,' because her husband Charles ran a full-time dental practice. Helen had given up her work as a pharmacist to manage the ranch. It took several trips over the mountains in her underpowered Volkswagen truck. To get up the steepest hills she would gun the engine on the flats and hope no one got in her way before she reached the top. The Bacigalupi family still grow grapes and starting with their third generation, they opened their own winery and tasting room, run by the twin granddaughters. The site of those original vines is on a low rise behind the tasting room. When I first visited years ago, they were still there and producing. But since then, the family replanted with new vines to support the next generation.

While that's a delightful story, the source of the rest of the grapes that went in those bottles is just as interesting. Most of the Chardonnay in Napa is grown in Los Carneros along the northern edge of the bay, with some good 'Chard' vineyards as far up as the Oak Knoll district, just south of Yountville. The upper valley is not only too hot, but it's so ideal for the expensive red Bordeaux grapes that Cabernet and Merlot take precedence.

The Napa vineyard where Mike Grgich found the rest of his Chard was at Muir Hanna, on the southwestern edge of Oak Knoll, at the foot of *basaltic* Mount Veeder. If the name Muir sounds familiar, then you may have visited Muir Woods, the famous redwood forest, a short ride up the coast from San Francisco.

John Muir was a naturalist and botanist whose research, lobbying efforts and friendship with President Theodore Roosevelt led to the establishment of the national parks system. We can thank him for Yosemite, which was the first National Park, and for founding the Sierra Club, a friend to tree lovers everywhere. His descendants farm a lovely vineyard in the southwest corner of Napa Valley just ten minutes from downtown.

I took clients there one day for a tasting having no idea of the family connection. But then I noticed two beautiful, period landscape paintings hanging on the wall in their living room. Being a lover of art, I asked them about the two scenes. That's when I found out who their great-grandfather was. Muir had mentored the painter, introducing him to Yosemite, and received the two paintings in thanks.

Was the 'Judgement' fair to the French, especially considering that a competition was not the original intention? It's true that Spurrier had included twice as many American wines as French, because he was anxious to show off what they had found on their trip to California. On the other hand, the tasting took place in Paris with all French judges, so the French wines enjoyed a home field advantage, or rather, a home palate advantage.

Based on their previous experiences, they could assume that the best wines were French. What they didn't figure on was the near ideal climatic and geologic conditions for growing wine grapes that the Americans enjoyed. The Californian's also had some very resolute and highly skilled people who believed in their vineyards' potential, and that was enough!

Did this 'Judgement' signal an immediate shift in the global wine world? *No!* The French, Italians and Germans were going to continue to buy the bottles that were filled down the lane from their homes, because that's what they had always done! But that article on the front page of the Times did tell the quickly growing number of American wine lovers, buyers and restaurants, that those guys and gals in California could make wines every bit as good as the French, at reasonable prices.

What they didn't foresee was that wine consumption the United States would almost *triple* since that time. They also didn't reckon on the effect that the American's dedication to research, technology and innovation would have on winemaking worldwide. The American's willingness to share that knowledge would gradually bend the standards that we use when we evaluate wine in their direction.

Chapter Eight
The Mexican Heritage

In the 1960's and 1970's, when new money started coming into the North Bay Wine Country, there were almost no Mexican families living there. That should seem odd since this region was *part of Spain,* and then Mexico, for longer than it's been part of the United States. Even though growing wine grapes has been an occupation here for generations, since the end of Prohibition, the work was done by farmers sitting on their tractors. They planted vines wide enough that there was plenty of room between the rows for their *'John Deere.'*

The only time Mexican workers came here was to pick the fruit, whether it was plums, walnuts or wine grapes. In those days, the grapes that the locals grew mostly went into what the industry calls jug wines, inexpensive vintages made in big commercial wineries and sold in large bottles under a variety of labels.

Then in the 1970's that model began to change. We'd like to think that was due to the famed "Judgment of Paris" tasting, which showed off the California wines in such a spectacular way. Many believe that it kicked off the renaissance, but there were many other factors that transformed this region from a producer of jug wines to a premium wine destination. If the growing conditions are equal, the main difference between an inexpensive wine, and a price tag that makes you *catch your breath*, is the number of times that workers go into the vineyard to tend the plants.

Yes, there are factors in location and microclimates that determine whether a vineyard has the potential to produce wonderful grapes, and yes, the North Bay is one of the best places. But, once that is recognized and the owner commits to planting the vines, the difference comes down to how many times someone looks at each vine and does what needs to be done.

For a vineyard owner, every time a team goes between the vines, it *costs them money*. After that, any difference in quality comes down to how much fruit they are willing to reject to make sure only the best goes into their bottles and how well the weather supports their work.

But *it all starts* in the vineyard, which is a field of berry bushes. Once they're planted, they'll start producing fruit after about three years. Then they'll continue producing grapes for twenty, thirty, forty or more years, depending on the grape variety and the vagaries of the market and disease. A grower of grapes for bulk wines will send machinery into the vineyard five times a year. A premium producer might send teams of workers into the vineyard *ten, or even twenty times* a year, often with hand tools for pruning, grafting and picking.

For large scale work, a small vineyard might turn to a management company, but they'll have one or two workers who are continually doing this and that to keep the vines happy. Only the largest vineyards typically have a full-time team capable of doing all the work.

In the North Bay wine region, the typical vineyard is ten to twenty acres. A large vineyard of five hundred acres will require about twenty workers. To put this in perspective, in the central valley where the bulk wine grapes are grown today, *entirely* using machinery, a 20-acre vineyard would be a hobby farm. But the premium growers in the North Bay can earn five or ten times more per ton for their grapes than in the Central Valley, because of much better growing conditions, although with smaller yields.

It's hard to beat the North Bay's weather. It alternates between hot, dry, incredibly bright days in the ideal eighty-degree range, followed by cool, foggy nights that preserve the acid in the grapes, and provide the vines with just the right amount of water. As it became obvious that great grapes could be grown here, vineyard owners started looking for full time workers who had the necessary skills. As a result, the North Bay vineyard teams are among the *highest* paid agricultural workers in the country. As more wineries began turning out premium wines, the demand for full-time workers grew. Those young Mexican men who came here to pick grapes during harvest time, started finding full time positions at the vineyards, and made this their home. Well, young men with good jobs attract young women, and so their girlfriends and wives came north from Mexico.

Then their babies were born here in Northern California and grew up speaking English and Spanish and translating for their parents. As the grapes began earning more per ton, the workers' skills became more valuable to the growers, along with their need to hold onto folks who would develop a relationship with the vineyards that they tended year after year.

Working in the vineyards is hard and the vines are often low to the ground, requiring a great deal of bending. It requires a hearty constitution and bodies accustomed to agricultural work. Fortunately, the Mexican workers tended to be compact and tough, making them suited to tending the vines.

But it is not about brute strength. When it comes to the pruning, the *crews of women* are among the highest paid, because their dexterity is critical to attaining superior results. The way they prune the vines affects the next two years of production and there is *no undo button* once the canes fall to the ground. As wineries became more successful, they added more full-time workers, and when vineyards changed hands the workers familiar with that land normally stayed on. There are world renowned vineyards in the North Bay that have been cared for by three generations of the same family, originally from Mexico.

Convincing vines to produce superior fruit is a demanding process, and the workers are diligently trained. They often come up through a familial mentoring system when nieces and nephews get jobs thanks to an uncle or aunt's recommendation. That means that they have the dual pressure of being under the eyes of both their boss and their Tio or Tia, who knows that this kid's performance reflects on them. Many of the workers we see in the vineyards send a large part of their weekly pay home to Mexico.

The vineyard manager or consultant develops the strategy that the team then implements, and learning all the steps and techniques required in their work takes time. In the springtime, soon after the first leaves appear, they sucker the vines, trimming away any leaves on the long woody stock. That both promotes more vigorous growth on the canopy above and limits the potential of insects climbing up the vine from the ground. As the new canes spring out, workers will walk between the vines and weave the flexible wood into the wires above.

That way the vine can take full advantage of the sunshine while limiting the amount of shade that falls on the developing grapes below. As the vines fill out, workers may trim away any leaves shading the thick-skinned grapes like Cabernet Sauvignon or leave them in place if they need to protect the delicate, thin skin varieties, like Pinot Noir, from the hot sun. You'll see *both men and women* out between the vines soon after dawn, and they'll often spend most of the day working in the bright, hot sun. Fortunately, California is a place that values its workers, so due to state regulations, when it's over ninety degrees, work stops in the vineyards. They pitch tents in the vineyard provide shade for breaks, and insulated jugs of icy water to keep them hydrated.

At harvest time you can always tell when the pickers have moved through the vines by the line of leaves on the ground, and the yellowing leaves around where the grapes had been hanging. You can practically see the plants relax as they are relieved of their load, and soon after, the green leaves will turn golden yellow.

In the *wintertime rainy season,* the winds will shake the leaves off the vines and work will stop in the vineyards. This is when the workers customarily visit their families in Mexico for the Christmas holiday. But after the New Year they'll return because there's work that needs to be done, pruning away last year's canes and preparing the vines for the coming season.

In recent years, the demand for workers has grown so high that as soon as the leaves are off the vines from the first blustery wintertime rains, lines of workers cars will appear alongside the vineyards, as the teams head in between the vines with their tools in hand.

But those wintertime rains can bring work to a halt because the tractors running through the mud can tear up carefully groomed rows, and trimming vines when they are wet makes them vulnerable to fungus. If conditions merit, the workers paint the cut tips with a gray green fungicide to forestall any problems. As the winter stretches on, we watch patches of vineyards, here and there trimmed back to the sturdy wood. And in the

Springtime, there will always be the odd vineyard where last year's canes are still intact, with tiny green leaves sprouting along their willowy length. It makes you wonder, was the owner late paying last year's contractor bill, or did they forget to schedule a crew, or are they planning to rip out the vines, so they didn't bother with the pruning? Usually, it's the latter!

This region has suffered from a string of devasting fires, so many of the Mexican men found jobs in construction rebuilding burnt houses. Meanwhile others went to work for the now legal cannabis growers. As a result, it's become increasingly hard to find vineyard workers.

Fifty years after the Judgment of Paris, the children of that first generation aren't doing that work, because they went to the local colleges and the state's Universities, learning the art and science of wine.

They are the winery managers, winemakers, executives and owners. At Napa County College, with its world class wine production program, forty percent of the students are bilingual in English and Spanish. So, the region depends on new workers coming from Mexico.

It is fortunate that there are more workers on hand during harvest than at any other time because during the late summer fires of 2017, 2019 and 2020 they went back and forth from *picking grapes to fighting the fires*. It is helpful to understand that California farmers know how to fight fires and the same bulldozers, water trucks and shovels they use for developing vineyards, work just as well for cutting fire breaks and soaking hotspots.

The 2017 fire broke out at night in high winds, right in the middle of harvest. The first week, before the fire companies arrived with their helicopters and flying water tankers, the local police and fire companies were entirely involved with moving people out of the path of the flames. But, *from the first day,* the local ranchers and their teams split their time between picking the fruit and fighting the flames. It was their toughness and determination that prevented the fire from becoming a catastrophe.

Wine Country is always evolving, and the biggest change is in how the winery tasting rooms changed due to COVID. During that period the wineries, which are food producers, stayed open. They could see a limited number of appointments, hosted outside, often on brand new patio furniture. But the real transformation in the tasting rooms took place in the staff. Before the shutdown, *'Boomers'* made up about forty percent of the tasting room staff. In some tasting rooms it was more like one hundred percent gray hairs.

These were people who had retired from other jobs and wanted a part-time job to get them out of the house. It was fun, not very strenuous and the wineries loved them because they didn't demand much in pay, or benefits, and they were very patient with the customers, which is important in wine sales. But when COVID began it ravaged that generation and they were all sent home. Well, the thing about the Boomers is that they are very resourceful. They were raised by 'The Greatest Generation' who expected a lot from them. So, when they went home, they *found other things to do*; starting businesses, getting involved with their grandkids, or volunteering.

When the tasting rooms reopened, they called their former employees to come back, and only about one in ten Boomers returned. The wineries were in a jam. They had been paying peanuts for part-time workers when no appointments were required. Now every tasting was *by appointment, and more expensive,* and they needed dependable help. To get workers to apply, they doubled what they previously paid and offered full-time jobs with benefits and commissions.

Suddenly the young people who had grown up in this region, many with Mexican parents who worked in the industry, for the first time took a serious look at these jobs. They would never have touched them before, with their part-time hours and low pay. But now they saw the opportunity to work in the industry that was part of their family tradition for good pay. It also meant not having to travel outside the area to get a decent paying job. When they started their new positions, they saw that most of their co-workers were also young, which meant they were able to work with potential friends and partners.

This solved a major problem that the wineries had been struggling with for many years. The clientele in the tasting rooms was getting older, and they were buying less wine. They needed to attract younger customers who would develop a loyalty to the brand and buy their wines for many years to come. Suddenly they saw that having a younger team in the tasting room was attracting younger customers. Also, many of the new team members are *bilingual in English and Spanish,* which means they are attracting another sizable demographic, the Spanish speakers.

It turns out that all the wineries needed to do to solve their demographic challenge in the tasting room was to endure a major pandemic. Clearly this is a case where a box of lemons became a pitcher of tasty limoncello.

How is this going to change the future of wine country, as these young Mexican Americans become increasingly knowledgeable about the business of wine? It is inevitable that their customer sales experience and evolving opinions will shape the future of the region, which is only right sincethe Mexican traditions are so much a part of its past.

Afterthought: The Fans

Move To a Vineyard, It Will Be Romantic...!

We got into the winery tour business quite by accident. We had attended a conference in San Francisco 18 months before and stayed on for a sorely needed vacation. The idea of writing a book about winery buildings from a Feng Shui perspective was the project that inspired us to move 3,000 miles from Philadelphia to Wine Country. It had only taken us 18 months to wrap up the ongoing certification classes we were teaching and figure out the logistics of this coast-to-coast move. Once we settled in, we started our research. It was a fun process because we were, after all, in Wine Country, and we already had a great deal of interest, and a little knowledge about wine. As we made personal connections with a few winemakers and winery owners, our 'buildings book' idea took shape.

We *first* moved to Sonoma for our research and Ralph was out every few days visiting wineries, meeting key people, photographing buildings and developing content. Winery people are a chatty bunch, and they love the idea of inspiring a book. In addition to winemakers and owners, he ran into more than a few tour guides. Then he got the brilliant idea to take a part time job driving wine tours. Why not get paid for a little on-the-job research?

This smart move got him *up close and personal* at a huge number of wineries, talking to people who were grateful for the customers he brought. In the course of his interviews, a secondary theme began to evolve. These winery folks were asking for a 'connect-the-dots' type of tour book to answer visitors' questions about where to eat, where to stay, which winery would they recommend and more. Now, Ralph has a great feel for sales and can't ignore the interests of the 'marketplace.'

As the 'building book' *morphed* into a tour book, we became more and more connected with hotels and wineries, especially in Napa. When opportunities opened up there, we realized it was time to move closer to our connections. Friends suggested different areas and options in Napa, and all of them were very close to the vineyards, something we did not have nearby in Sonoma.

How cool would that be? Living a stone's throw from the wineries that Ralph was visiting with his guests. "Move to a vineyard," they said. "It will be romantic," they said. After an extensive search, we moved in July and found an idyllic spot near the Oak Knoll AVA with beautiful vineyards and wineries a block away. Perfect...!

Fast forward to a Winter night in late March, cozy in our bed at 3AM, when suddenly we hear what could only be a *'bevy of helicopters'* hunting down a crime suspect in our quiet little part of paradise. We say 'bevy' because we were used to the occasional copter in the middle of the night due to being close to a hospital with an emergency helipad. "What is going on?" The sound sort of came and went, like waves of aircraft heading to the west. Could they be squadrons from Travis Air Force Base? If so, something big was happening.

"Turn on the air cleaner... where are my ear plugs... no, throw on some clothes, we have to go out and get to the *bottom* of this." By this time, it was 5 am. "I'll buy you a Starbucks! We have to see what's going on."

If you have been to Wine Country, you may have noticed those big fan-looking things in the middle of some vineyards. We encountered them in Sonoma and when we asked, they said, "Oh, those are frost fans, but they aren't really used anymore." Well, maybe not in Sonoma but they are everywhere in frostier Napa. And when overnight temps get close to freezing around the time of bud break, they certainly use them. Wineries will not let a whole vineyard of expensive Cabernet vines freeze-dry before they can make their expensive wine. The noisy motors are droning enough, but they also oscillate, adding to that whirring sound that left our brains buzzing.

You know how people have that pet that destroys everything, or yips incessantly and you often wonder, 'Why do they keep that pet?" Well, we understand why now, because we still live in paradise in ear shot of the fans, and we know where they keep the ear plugs at the local Orchard Supply store. And now we know why they carry so many.

We hope you enjoy this book as much as we have enjoyed writing it. And come visit us out here in Wine Country!

Lahni & Ralph DeAmicis found their way from speaking and writing about design and health into also speaking and writing about Wine Country, by starting to write a book about winery buildings. As they researched the topic, they realized there were no local 'winery' tour books, so the project morphed into their first guidebook. That series, now in its seventh edition, continues to be the region's most popular.

Eventually they started Amicis Tours which has taken them, and their clients, to many beautiful places and opened doors for them into the wine industry. Their TV show 'Wine Country at Work' and their documentary film series explore this fascinating region. They share stories about the region with visiting groups. They also do speeches and team building about using the Power of ErgoDynamic Design to improve lives and work performance, with an admittedly Wine Country filter.

www.SpaceAndTime.com

Other Titles by The Authors

A Tour Guide's Napa Valley
A Tour Guide's Sonoma Wine Country
Sonoma Navigator, Maps & Highlights
Napa Navigator, Maps & Highlights
Napa Valley Winery Maps
Sonoma Winery Maps

PlanetaryCalendar.com
Published Annually since 1949

Planetary Calendar Astrology Forecasts & Health Hints
Two Wall Sizes, a Pocket Size, a Day Planner &
a Digital Version for your Phone and Computer
The Lunar Food and Wine Tasting Calendar
The Companion Book
'Planetary Calendar Astrology,
Moving Beyond Observation to Action'
Coming Soon
Reclaiming Astrology from the Patriarchy
The Story of the Stolen Zodiac

From the 'Tango' Series
Feng Shui and the Tango, The Dance of Design
Feng Shui and the Tango, The Essential Chapters
25th Anniversary Edition
FS&T Prosperity Lessons
FS&T Happiness Lessons
The Dream Desk Quiz
The Clutter Bug's Emergency Handbook

Find their books and documentaries at:
www.WineCountryInShorts.com

www.ingramcontent.com/pod-product-compliance
Lightning Source LLC
LaVergne TN
LVHW012025060526
838201LV00061B/4466